FISHING IN THE SUN

...And the rain, wind & snow

COPYRIGHT 2020 © MIKE KERNAN

COVER DESIGN: Ryan McGinness
COVER PHOTO: Jim Patrick
WEBSITE: www.mikekernan.co.uk

JBM19
BOOKS

FISHING IN THE SUN

MIKE KERNAN

JBM19
BOOKS

ABOUT THE AUTHOR

MIKE KERNAN has been fishing for more than 50 years, pursuing everything from sticklebacks to sharks across Scotland and far beyond. He has been writing an angling column for The Scottish Sun since 2008. After an award-winning career in newspapers and television, Glasgow-born Mike is now an author, university tutor and grandad. Visit www.mikekernan.co.uk for pictures from his fishing adventures and more info about his writing projects.

ALSO BY MIKE KERNAN

The Fenian

Contents

TO PAUL

No better fishing company

Introduction

EVERY now and then I make a resolution to become a better angler, mainly for the right reasons, like enhancing my knowledge and adding to my skill set. Self-improvement if you like, which is surely a good thing. But it's also partly so I can stop envying those anglers – and there are many – who not only consistently catch more fish than me, but go about it in a way that seems instinctive and effortless.

There is also an element of wanting to feel less useless and OK, maybe less embarrassed, in the company of those much better fishermen. Like the boat partner a year or two back who hit a trout every other cast as we drifted next to the sailing club at Rutland, while I worked my butt off for the odd offer even though we had the same fly on and I was trying to replicate what he was doing.

Or the legendary Scotland international who casually

spotted 10 fish to my one on Carron one evening.

"Four o' clock, Mike, 20 yards," he'd say helpfully, and I would stare cluelessly at blank, anonymous water.

I know what I should be doing to get to the next level. I should be reading all the books and studying the rivers, lochs and shores like I was doing a university degree. I should be risking a divorce by installing an aquarium full of snails and shrimps in my kitchen so I can learn their dance moves.

I should be picking the brains of those much better anglers until they get so fed up that they take out a restraining order to keep me at a safe distance. I should be out fishing every spare second, doing it again and again and again until I can't help but learn something.

There is one major problem, though. Well, two actually. Firstly, I like my fishing the way it is. I'm relaxed about it. More often than not, I catch one or two, or a few, or sometimes even a lot and I go home perfectly satisfied. I don't fret that I should have caught more or even, now and again, that I haven't caught at all.

So, do I really want to make that leap to the next level? I suppose it's a bit like the 24-handicap golfer who loves the game but every so often dreams of being as good as his mate who plays off five. But he isn't sure he wants to go as far as taking lessons from the club pro and having to worry about tucking his elbow in half a centimetre because his tee shot is drifting fractionally to the left.

Secondly, and this is the crux of it, I don't take fishing seriously enough. It's not my job. It's a hobby, a pastime, what I do for fun, the part of my life when I can forget all the serious stuff. If you think words like hobby and pastime don't do fishing justice, then call it a sport. But that only reinforces my point because sport is, primarily, something to enjoy, right?

If we agree that fishing is a sport, then thankfully it is one that doesn't come with all the tribal baggage which, again, means we don't have to take it too seriously. I've yet to find a fish that asks what school you went to before it decides whether or not to eat your maggots or bite your spinner. And who cares what team a guy supports when he is handing you the killer fly on the dam wall?

While I'm on the subject, the best story I ever heard about all that nonsense in a fishing context was about the guy who invented the Ally McCoist fly. I really hope this tale is true and not urban myth. Apparently, he hadn't yet given it a name by the time he took it for a swim at Wellsfield fishery in Stirlingshire. With its olive fritz and gold flash in the tail, the lure was nailing trout after trout and was clearly the star of the show. Two other anglers wandered over for a chat and asked him what he was catching on. Without hesitation, he handed them one each and, knowing they were Celtic fans, came up with the Ally McCoist on the spot – purely as a wind-up. I love that.

It goes without saying that the name didn't stop them using it. After all, what's a little thing like football loyalty when there are fish to be caught? That, thankfully, is about as serious as football and religion get in our game and another reason why I love it so much.

Same goes for politics. Which party gets your X in the box every four or five years means hee-haw when there's a bunch of you sitting on a boat rocking on the waves as you wait in solidarity for the first rod tip to start trembling.

All of which has made fishing, for me at least, an escape from all the division and angst and horror and hate and showbiz trivia that occupied much of my mind when I was doing my day job as a journalist for the best part of half a century.

The reason I am telling you all of this, my failure to get overly earnest about angling or immerse myself too deeply in the nuts and bolts, is that I am obliged to give you fair warning about this book. You know, like the alerts that pop up before telly programmes, telling you the show you are about to watch contains scenes of sex and violence that some viewers might find upsetting.

(BTW, is it just me that suspects these notices are actually meant to draw in viewers rather than the other way about, like the old Channel Four red triangle that anyone of a certain vintage will remember?)

Where was I? Oh yes, the warning about this book. Actually, there is a little sex and violence but not enough to have old Uncle Hector reaching for his heart pills, and that's not what I'm on about anyway.

Basically, you need to be aware that this is not, repeat not, a How-To book. You are not going to be granted some Harry Potter cloak of angling invincibility by reading it. You are not going to find out how to catch more fish, learn how to build complicated rigs or get a free kit for your very own worm farm in the loft. Neither does this book contain any of those puzzling diagrams of knots that look like snakes playing Twister.

If you were expecting that kind of thing, then you probably want to go and check out the Amazon returns policy or else stick the book away as a stocking filler for some less fussy fishing relative.

There is no mystery as to why this is not a How-To book. First and foremost, I am not an expert. I am an enthusiast and the point of this book is to reflect my own personal take on fishing as, hopefully, some of you will have discovered and maybe even enjoyed in my Scottish Sun column over the last dozen years.

To my mind, fishing should be fascinating, exciting, thought-provoking, bursting with incidents and characters and, above all, good fun. The same goes for this book.

So instead of catching and tackle advice, in these pages you will find serial killers, a zombie kid and brushes with death from the Galloway Forest to the frozen wastes of Finland. You will meet a 2000-year-old angling cheat, a Spanish hippy trading his girlfriend for a mullet and the fishing equivalent of Archie McPherson.

I've dipped into the memory banks for a tour of some of Scotland's top trout fisheries as well as trips to the Faroes and the Hebrides. I also reveal the big untold fishing secrets of the 2020 lockdown.

And talking of secrets, I might even break the How-To promise briefly to let you in on the ultimate hush-hush wisdom about never blanking again in your entire life.

However good, bad, exciting or difficult the fishing, the constant through every chapter of this book is not so much the catching or the species or the size or the conditions or the scenery, but the company. When I look back through my fishing years, adventures and travels, what I think of most fondly are the characters, the friendships, the laughter, the advice, the acts of generosity, kindness and craziness.

There are a few people, therefore, that I need to mention

for their roles in making my fishing definitely more enjoyable and, occasionally, more productive. To varying degrees, they helped make this book possible:

My father, for first putting a fishing rod in my hands.

My grandfather, who saw the awful bird's nest I'd got my line into as a youngster at the canal and used a phrase that I didn't understand then and don't understand now, but have used regularly ever since – "You're in a worse state than Russia."

The anonymous Arbroath charter boat skipper who gave me a piece of advice when I was eight or nine that has stood me in good stead my whole life.

The equally anonymous Englishman whose five-minute crash course in coarse fishing stopped me from chucking it altogether at the age of 10.

My old pal, Andy Johnstone, who introduced me to fly fishing when I lived in Galloway more than 30 years ago.

Another old mate, Alan McGowan, who got me back into fly fishing on one of our numerous trips. You know, we really should have written that Angus and Morag sitcom.

George Murray, who grew from fishery boss to close friend. He has been there for me when it counted more than once.

Stephen McCaveny, at tackle giants Daiwa. Without his support, The Scottish Sun fishing column would probably not have reached its first birthday.

My creative son-in-law, Ryan McGinness, for a cracker of a book cover and a slick website, even if I have to be dragged kicking and screaming to update it.

My ever-patient wife Margaret, not just for the constant

encouragement, but for sometimes letting me talk about fishing for as long as 30 seconds before putting up a hand and saying: "Right, I'm bored now."

I'm not even going to attempt to name all the boat partners, fly tiers, fishery owners, fellow anglers and newspaper column contacts who have generously shared their time, expertise and good company. I would be bound to miss some people out because at times my memory is as poor as my choice of fly. That would be unforgiveable.

But they can all be assured of one thing – if my skills have not improved as much as they should have for their intervention, the blame is entirely mine. Problem is, I just don't take fishing seriously enough.

Mike Kernan, November 2020.

Chapter 1

Scary monsters

SERIAL killers, certain death on the rocks, Rip Van Winkle goes pike fishing. Yup, fishing can have its episodes of genuine fear, its serious squeaky bum moments. But none of those tops my scariest memory of all. Nah, that honour goes to a three-year-old girl.

Just to clear up the first lot. Thankfully, I have never actually bumped into a slavering, blade-wielding maniac on the banks of a lonely loch – the type worthy of his own six-part Netflix series. No, The Tiger Trout King, or The Fly-Rod Ripper, or The Keepnet Killer, as he might have been known, was the creation of a non-fishing pal of mine with an overactive imagination.

I need to point out that Kenny is a town boy through and

through. The kind of guy who thinks cows and sheep are wild animals and an urban golf course is the heart of the countryside. For Kenny, grass is the green bit on Match of the Day and trees are for hanging decorations on at Christmas. Ask him where to find fish and he'll tell you the chip shop or the frozen aisle at ASDA.

So, usual Monday coffee machine chat and he asked in a not-really-that-interested-just-making-conversation way if I had been out fishing at the weekend. I got that a lot when I was on the paper full-time, because of my column. I caught a look of surprise and something resembling mild panic when I told him I'd had a cracking session the night before. So good, in fact, that I was still catching at nearly midnight.

"Er, but…but it must have been dark, surely?"

Well, naturally, I said, but it was high summer and the fish were more active than they had been in the heat of the day and there were still flies hatching so you've got to take advantage of these things. Course, I'd have been as well trying to explain Einstein's theory or the latest Brexit deal or no deal. The technical details didn't even make it in the first ear never mind out the other. No, Kenny had other concerns.

"You weren't out at that time on your own, were you?"

Actually, I had been, at least for the last couple of hours. One of the other club members I'm pally with hadn't been feeling that great and chucked it about tennish. There might still have been one bloke away over on the far side but he had faded out of sight as the last remnants of light slipped away.

"Were you not crapping it, out there in the middle of

9

nowhere in the dark on your lonesome?"

To be truthful, there was a time when fishing in the deep black of night used to play tricks with my psyche. They say noises are magnified at night or maybe that's all in the head. But there is no question you can get unnerved by simple things like the creaking of a branch, the deep lowing of a cow caught on the breeze from a distant field, a wave slapping on the rock down to your right. All these sounds are suddenly much clearer and more stark at night.

But I solved any lingering, primal fear of the dark by the same method I used to calm my kids when they were younger and they came to a frightening scene in a telly programme or film. I made it ordinary and mundane. I'd tell them to remember that just next to where that giant was about to snatch the princess's baby, there were cameras on trolleys and folk holding microphones and they probably had to film the scene eight times because the actor playing the giant felt so ridiculous in his gruesome make-up that he couldn't stop giggling. I worked in television news for a few years so I was able to chuck in some jargon to make my calming words sound more authentic.

In much the same way, I make the darkness ordinary when I'm out fishing late. I remind myself that I am standing in exactly the same place where I'd felt comfortable and relaxed just 20 minutes or half an hour ago, except the landscape is now in different, more sombre clothing.

But Kenny's fevered imagination was still in overdrive. And remember, this is an experienced national newspaper reporter who has faced down gangsters and police chiefs. An intelligent professional, supposedly.

"You not scared there might be serial killers at that time of night?"

Hmm, wasn't sure where to start with that one. Did he mean a lone serial killer, but was just using the plural because he didn't want to offend by singling one out, just in case there was another one lurking behind the office coffee machine? Or did he think there was a kind of club or association for serial killers where they kept in touch, swapped notes and advice and handed out madman-of-the-month awards? Then, maybe once or twice a year, they get together for a convention and hold it at midnight on the banks of the loch where I happen to be fishing.

Perhaps I was wrong and really was putting myself at serious risk, though. Maybe Kenny's right and that is exactly how a serial killer's mind works.

Right, time for victim number seven. I'm accelerating now and the dogged detective pursuing me is waiting for me to slip up so I need to throw him off the scent. I know, I'll wait till midnight then take a run down to that remote trouty place on the west coast and see if there's anyone daft enough to be out fishing on his own at the witching hour. Serves them right for staying out so late if I go all Hannibal Lecter on them.

No Kenny, all things considered, the fear of serial killers doesn't weigh too heavily on my mind when I'm fishing in the dark...unless I really did hear someone say *Here's Johnny* behind that tree over there.

The death on the rocks one though, now that was a more serious and realistic possibility. Whether you are a freshwater or sea angler, the chances are you will have flirted with disaster on a boat at least once in your fishing

11

career.

We were on one of my favourite Hebridean lochs, doing a decent job of not disturbing the resident brownies overly much on a warm, clammy day in May. We had been fishing hard for days, from dawn till what passes for a fleeting dusk in this part of the country at that time of year, and minimal sleep was starting to take its toll.

My fishing pal Alan decided to shut his eyes for five minutes – a snooze which rapidly turned into a full-blown coma complete with John Deere soundtrack. Huh, no stamina these thirty-something-year-olds. To be fair, he had been on the oars almost all day due to my staggering lack of co-ordination which means that on the rare occasions when he lets me row, our drift tends to be confined to a not very wide but perfect circle.

But fine, let him snooze. I was into one of those hypnotic casting rhythms that becomes strangely enjoyable even if you are getting only the odd flicker of interest which, to be honest, was something of an exaggeration.

Problem was, it was so hypnotic that I was oblivious to the wind that had suddenly picked up as it does with frightening regularity in the Hebrides – and I was casting away from shore. What set off the alarm was hearing a splash behind me. So few fish had been exposing their eyes to the sun that I turned my head to see where the rise was so I could attempt an acrobatic twist and cast.

That was when I realised that we were on a collision course with ugly, jagged rocks about the size of wheely bins. It was also when I realised that Alan was now lying stretched out along the bottom of the boat, unconscious rather than asleep. Worse still, he was blocking any access to the oars. Even taking my lack of co-ordination into account, at that point a not very wide but perfect circle would have been a decidely better option to being smashed to pieces on the rocks.

If anyone could have heard me, they'd have thought I was doing a rather frantic impression of the annoying chant from that spoof wildlife thing that was on telly a few years back. You know, the show with the talking animals that at least one person in your office still thinks is funny when they try it out on any colleague with the appropriate name.

"Alan, Alan, Alan," I yelled.

Finally, with just a few yards to spare and me praying hard that I wasn't going to have to put my lifejacket's newly expired three-year warranty to the test, he leapt up, grabbed the oars and steered us to safety. Hope I didn't kick you too hard, old pal.

Course, I can't really be too tough on Alan for drifting into the land of nod while out fishing. I did it myself once and the consequences were not just frightening but potentially fatal.

It was a cold, bleak winter's Sunday in mid-December, that part of the year when the Scottish days aren't so much short as merely a lesser shade of darkness for a brief hour or two in the middle. But I hadn't been out for a while and work had been a pain so I thought, sod it, a few hours pike fishing would be the perfect therapy to set me up for another grinding, short-staffed week, as well as the antidote to the previous day's interminable Christmas shopping.

I drove out to Spectacle Loch, a few miles into the Galloway Forest. Surrounded by pines, the loch gets its name because it is shaped like, er, a pair of spectacles, and

I'd caught some nice pike there in the past. Nothing huge mind, but fish of eight or nine pounds would turn up now and again and a pike of that size will give you a decent workout. In addition, the loch was rammed with perch which would provide some entertaining diversion while I waited for the bigger stuff to come along.

The obvious option, the sensible option, would have been to stick to the bank closest to the road. A couple of dozen yards from car to bank and I could have settled down quite comfortably and passed an easy, enjoyable few hours with, if I was lucky, a lean, mean winter pike as the bonus.

But then who takes the easy option when you've got your eye on the prize? Aside from the convenient closest bank being comparatively over-fished, the reed beds on the far side had been where I'd caught my best pike from Spectacle. So, off I plodded, carting rods, bag, landing net and fishing seat. The boggy route across to the far bank was manageable enough in daylight, when you could actually pick out the dry bits amid the oozing quagmire, so reaching my chosen spot wasn't a problem.

Fine, got myself settled and parked a nice, juicy strip of herring a yard or so out from the reeds about six feet beneath a big yellow float. Knowing how shallow the loch was, that would mean the bait sitting just off the bottom. I sprayed half a dozen handfuls of maggots into the water in an arc to see if I could stir up the perch then settled into my seat for a pleasant little session.

My immediate thought when I woke up in bed that night was that the room was colder than usual. Almost freezing, in fact. Well, it was winter and maybe my wife had left the window open as she likes a bit of cool air at night, no matter the temperature. No problem, I'll just burrow myself deeper into the duvet and drift off again. Except there was no duvet. Or pillow for that matter. Or even a bed. In fact, I wasn't even lying down. I was somewhere between sitting and slumped. And wait a minute, why is it so dark in here? Why isn't there at least some dim light from the street lamps in the main street outside? Could there be a power cut in the town?

In retrospect, I think this might be what is known as being disorientated. It was probably only a minute or two but it felt like an awful long time before the truth dawned and I figured it out. It was pitch black, as in struck-blind pitch black. I was chilled right into my bones. I was outdoors, I was out fishing and I'd turned into Rip Van Winkle in the Galloway Forest.

Right. Stop. Don't panic. Think it through. Where am I? Oh yeah, Spectacle. How long have I been asleep? Look at your watch. Forget it, can't see the damned thing. Doesn't really matter anyway. The important thing is to gather up the gear and get out of here. Wait, how many rods have I got and where the hell are they? OK, two rods. Feel around, then reel them in and break the rods down. What else have I got with me? Landing net. Where is it? Nope, can't feel it on the ground around me. Tough, leave it and come back for it tomorrow. Bag? Here it is. Shove the tackle in any old way and sort it out when you get home. Right, think I've got everything except the net. But hang on, how do I get through that bog and what direction am I going in anyway?

I had visions of my missus finally noticing I wasn't there at some point that evening – or maybe in the next day or three – then a rescue party being assembled, perhaps even a helicopter with searchlight on full beam. But then I went off on another panic tangent altogether. Did I even tell her or anybody else where I was going? Play it back. Hmm, probably not. The odds were that I'd chucked the gear in the boot then opened the front door and shouted: "Back in a few hours."

How would anyone find me? Would I be discovered in a week's time looking like some freakish semi-man with a glaikit expression and my frozen lower half sucked into a muddy pit?

So, baby steps. One foot forward at a time, pressing into the ground gingerly to see if it was solid. I say forward, but it might have been left or right, or even backwards for all I knew. Then two passing cars in the distance saved me, which was very lucky because I'd seen only the occasional vehicle on that quiet forest road all day. The headlights from the first at least offered a clue as to where the road was and gave me a point to aim for. Much tentative edging and sucking boots out of the glue later, I made it to solid tarmac, with a final step as giant and important to me as Neil Armstrong's was to mankind. But where's the car? The second set of headlights showed it to me and the relief was huge.

Two lessons there. Number one, if you're fishing alone always make sure someone knows where you are going in case the worst happens. Number two, I know mobile phones can be a pain but never underestimate their value and make sure they are fully charged before you go. This incident happened in the days before smart phones became an extra limb. If something similar was to happen now, a phone could make the difference between life and death.

So yes, a few fear factors there but none to compare with the face-of-innocence little zombie who once sent an icy shiver right through me.

The scene was the River Gryffe in Renfrewshire. The time must have been around the start of the season because I knocked a wild brown trout on the head that day, which was very unusual for me. Back then I had a ritual of taking the first trout of the season home for my wife to eat, probably fulfilling some primal urge to go out hunting for the dinner. But that was my kill quota for the year and it's probably a sign of the times that I now feel the need to explain myself over the death of a single trout.

I had been drawn back to the Gryffe on a day permit by nostalgia. Many years before, when I lived in the area, I had joined the local angling club and spent many enjoyable days in pursuit of the brown trout as well as the odd grayling and the even rarer salmon. It is a river of contrasts, with quiet, languid stretches through soft countryside and woodland, others through the middle of villages like Bridge of Weir and Houston, where an audience of too-cool-for-school teenagers would often have to be tolerated once the nights got lighter. The river has an interesting mix of wide, sweeping glides and narrow fast runs. In other words, plenty of water with an array of challenges.

On this occasion, I revived my regular game plan from all those years ago. Park down at the green bridge in the housing estate in Houston, hike a mile and a bit upstream past the hamlet of Crosslee, then step-and-cast my way back to the car. As it turned out, I could have saved myself the effort. I barely saw a fish and touched nothing all the way along the river till I reached one of my favourite old pools back at the start, or the finish, depending on how you look at these things.

Half an hour and I'd give it up as a fruitless day, I decided, as a bloke wandered down to the pool behind me and started setting up for bait fishing – the only other angler I had seen. He had a little girl with him, muffled up against the March chill, looking distinctly fed up and as if she'd had enough before he even got started.

You get the picture, don't you? Any angler who has ever had young kids in tow knows what this is all about. You're desperate to get out fishing but you have promised to look after the wee one, the missus hasn't got back from her mum's at the scheduled time and it will be dark in an hour or two. How bad can it be? All you have to do is keep an eye on the wean, make sure they don't drown, and you still get to cast a line. So you decide to take them fishing and have some "quality" time together.

The way the little girl was glancing around at first the ground, then at the river, told me she was just about at that stage where their minds make a small leap of logic. Stones. Water. Chuck. Splash. Repeat. It is lodged in every child's psyche. Did I say child's psyche? Huh, my wife would tell you, in an exasperated tone, that it's still lodged in mine.

Ah well, I thought, either I'll call it quits early or move back up river to that pool I missed out because it means an annoying squeeze through the jaggy bushes.

Then we were both distracted – the little girl and me – by the trout that grabbed the nymph I was letting swing into the slack water under the tree at the far bank. Nice sparkling fresh fish it was too, maybe a pound or a touch more. Perfect for the wife's annual Mike-caught meal. Job done.

Or so I thought.

The little girl had watched in rapt attention as I quickly subdued then netted the fish. Wide-eyed, she started to wander over, slowly at first, then with purpose.

"My name is Katherine-Anne, Kate for short," she announced herself. "I am three-years-old, four on my next birthday."

Not the shyest, most diffident kid I'd ever met, and she had even thrown in a free maths lesson.

"Can I see your fish please?" she asked with a mix of confidence and good manners.

The guy gave a shrug then called over, weakly and without a shred of conviction.

"C'mere Kate. Stop bothering the man."

What, pass up the chance of a few minutes' peace? Aye, very good pal.

I decided I'd better give him what I thought was a friendly and reassuring nod back, just so he'd know I wasn't some creep in the habit of attracting the attention of wee girls with Smarties, puppies or dead trout.

I laid the fish out on the grass and she hunkered down for a closer examination.

"Er, is it OK if I touch it?" she enquired, still the soul of politeness, and when I said that was fine, she began tracing circles round its red spots with her thumb. After running her index finger along its flank, I got the first clue that this was no ordinary child. A faint smile formed around her mouth and, with what sounded suspiciously like relish, she added: "It's very cold."

She puffed up her little cheeks and look squarely and seriously at me. Right, I thought, here comes the business end of the conversation.

"Can I have it?" she asked boldly.

I explained it was for my wife's dinner but told her that her dad would probably catch one soon. Then, just so I'd know how much it would mean to her and how ludicrous my attempt at reassurance was, she leaned her shoulders back a fraction and nodded in his direction but without bothering to look at him because we both knew fine who she was talking about.

She rolled her eyes contemptuously and said: "Huh, he's useless. He never catches any fish. And, he's not even my real dad."

The withering look and condescending tone seemed so beyond her years that I had a fleeting if illogical notion that she was really a 30-year-old munchkin at the wind-up. I tried again, saying that maybe he would get lucky this time because seriously, I didn't want to undermine the guy. But I did add that if I caught another one, she could have it for her tea.

Katherine Anne, Kate for short, seemed content with this arrangement and headed towards her stepdad, or mum's friend, or whatever he was to her, but she pulled up abruptly halfway and marched back towards me.

Her face was an expressionless mask as she pointed towards the fish and asked: "How did you dead it?"

It felt more like an interrogation now but given her age, I didn't want to be too graphic so I reached for an answer somewhere between factual and non-nightmare inducing. I pointed at the small hardwood tool next to my fishing bag and replied: "That thing's called a priest. I just gave the fish a little tap on the head with it."

She gave me the coldest look I have ever seen in any person, never mind a little girl, and asked: "Could you hit it again, really really hard, so I can see its blood?"

Never mind the trout's blood – mine ran cold. I felt I had no option but to pack up and go home, and though I couldn't swear to it, her head may have rotated through 180 degrees. Also, I couldn't get the theme from The Exorcist out of my head on the drive back.

Chapter 2

Smoke on the water

I CAN never drive past the road sign for Arbroath without breaking into a smile born of nostalgia. I used to see that sign regularly on my frequent trips up the A90 when my daughter lived in Aberdeen and I'd never fail to be struck by a flood of memories stored away for decades but still clear in the recollection. A pleasant reminder that a childhood holiday in the Angus seaside town was where fishing started for me all those years ago.

But at the same time, there is a little sting tucked in there too. A warning that sometimes precious memories are best not held up too closely to the light.

It's maybe hard to believe nowadays, particularly for youngsters, but families like mine from the West of

Scotland really did spend their main summer holiday in places like Arbroath. And Ayr and Girvan and Dunbar and Montrose and on and on. But back when I was a lad...sheesh, did I really just write that? What am I, a hundred and nine? But yes, back then, Arbroath was one of our regular holiday destinations and it was as exciting to us – my big sister and wee brothers – as I guess a fortnight in Tenerife or Turkey is to children nowadays.

These Scottish resorts, once thronged with families in shorts, sandals, brollies, plastic macs and pale, goose-pimpled flesh, are now the kind of places you might go to on a Sunday drive or more likely drive past on the way to somewhere else. Back then, in the mid-1960s, we didn't even have a car and I think that made it all the more of an adventure.

The blue No 159 into Buchanan Street, Glasgow, the rag-tag crocodile from the bus depot to Queen Street train station, which was mobbed with families like ours, all chattering and staring up with frantic anticipation at the destination board for their platform numbers. Then the journey up the east coast, always remembering to have a lucky penny ready to throw out the window when we crossed the Forth Bridge.

Like many kids, the harbour in Arbroath was a magnet to me. That sweet-sickly fishy tang, the white flash of swooping, squealing gulls, the bustle of fishing boats jostling for parking space, the calls and cries of trawlermen in their north-east sing-song. But most of all, I was drawn to the handful of men and boys fishing from the harbour walls, some kids flat on their stomachs as they peered down into the depths. Every now and then, somebody would swing up a fish and some of the boys would rush over for a look.

So, a chunk of my precious holiday savings went on a cheap, flimsy Winfield all-in-one fishing kit from Woolies to get me started. What sealed the deal was that amidst the shoals of what I now assume were little coalies, I once heaved out a monster…or at least it was to me. A decent sized flounder that to this day stars in a fading, black and white snap, gripped by a serious-faced wee boy who owned my childhood and my hair.

I remember too, fishing for hours from the rocks near the beach where it turned out that flounders like the one I'd thought a giant at the harbour, were ten a penny. The highlight was the excitement of hauling in a big pollock which had sneaked in and beaten the flatties to my bait, then dragging it through the shingle and past the sandcastle brigade to show off to my family.

It was all great salty sport of the kind you'd expect on a seaside holiday but funnily enough, what is most lodged in the memory banks is an introduction to brown trout that would spark off a lifelong fascination for what remains my favourite species.

The residents of the Brothock Water were typical Scottish burn brownies – small, easily spooked and, for me at least, impossible to catch as they darted for cover at the least movement. Looking back, it became a DIY course in reading and fishing a river in miniature. Working out how the current would carry the trout's food downstream and where the fish would lie in wait, ready to grab their meal with the least effort and danger. Learning the importance of cover and stillness.

I experimented with big hooks and little hooks, bubble floats or just a couple of split shot, scraps of bread, worms unearthed from under stones, even live insects which I suppose was a kind of crude introduction to fly fishing. I remember being given a piece of advice from a local worthy that I've never forgotten. He told me to try a *smaller* worm and explained: "If you've got a poke of chips, you don't just eat the big ones, do you?" I'm sure there was logic in there somewhere.

Then a kind of disbelief that melted into unbridled triumph when I finally got one. A moment when time seemed to stand still. Did I really just see my bubble float take a dip that wasn't caused by the current or the hook being caught on a weed? Was it really still being pulled under now? It wasn't until it shot across the burn attached to a trout that I took it all in. How proud I was to see it served up for breakfast by the landlady of our digs next morning, even if it stretched barely halfway across a tea plate.

It's a glorious memory that makes me wish I'd never stumbled across the Brothock on a flying visit to Arbroath about 10 or 12 years ago. But there it was: the wild, babbling, brownie-rich brook of my childhood, now just a sad trickle between two walls in the middle of town. I'm almost certainly being grossly unfair here. Chances are that if I'd had more time, I'd have easily located stretches of the burn more in tune with my childhood recollections. But then you know how the saying goes…nostalgia ain't what it used to be.

Back home, holiday over, I couldn't get fishing out of my head. The big snag was that the new town of

Cumbernauld, where I grew up, was pretty much as far from the sea as you can get in Scotland. That meant there was a shortage of harbours – and the place wasn't exactly overflowing with pristine trout streams either. There was the River Luggie and though I've heard of it being cleaned up and trout caught there in more recent times, my memory of it is of a glorified, murky ditch.

Other than that, there were a few clogged up trenches that weaved their way through the numerous building sites. They were only any good for catching sticklebacks in a bamboo cane net and filling a jam jar with tiny, helpless tiddlers that would turn belly up on your window sill by next morning.

But not far away, there was the canal – and it had actual fish in it at handy locations like Dullatur, Castlecary, Banknock and Auchinstarry. OK, the canal residents were not the darting, sparkling brown trout of the Brothock, but coarse species like perch and roach…and, fearsome as they seemed to a nine-year-old, pike.

My only problem was learning how to catch them and I became so used to not catching them that I might have given up fishing altogether if it hadn't been for my Crabtree moment.

For anyone who doesn't know, Mr Crabtree was the brainchild of a legendary angler, artist and writer by the name of Bernard Venables. His creation, the comic-strip adventures of a pipe-smoking fisher and, we assumed, his young son Peter, first appeared in a daily newspaper back in the 1960s and inspired a whole generation of anglers. You might have seen the concept brought beautifully back to life a few years ago by the infectious enthusiasm of the renowned John Bailey in TV's Fishing in the Footsteps of Mr Crabtree, even if our more politically correct times meant the pipe was nowhere to be seen.

I never did know the name of my own version of the character, but what I am certain of is that I owe him a massive debt. I came across him on the Forth and Clyde Canal when I was that struggling rookie angler. The fishing that had been such a source of fun and adventure on holiday was starting to lose its appeal because of that one vital missing ingredient – actually catching any fish.

It was on yet another day that was shaping up into the kind of miserable failure I had become so used to, that I rounded a bend and did a double take. *There's something wrong with this picture.* What I was looking at was an outsized green umbrella parked at the waterside with not a drop of rain in sight.

Underneath it, a man was perched on a stool, his eyes fixed on a tiny red tip no more than a foot from the end of his rod. He had mysterious boxes and tubs balanced on stands either side of him like a drum kit and the end of a round net sticking out of the water. The next puzzle was why he was chucking away handfuls of what I assumed was his bait. It took me and my pals hours to dig up enough worms for a day's fishing so the thought of chucking bait away was almost sinful.

But however odd it might have looked to my uneducated eye, whatever this bloke was doing was working. To my complete amazement, the float dipped under every few minutes. He'd quickly play a fish then swing it into his hand, before popping yet another one into what I soon found out was called a keepnet.

27

I approached, quietly and open-mouthed, trying to make sense of what I was witnessing. He gave me a friendly grin and in an accent that marked him out as coming from some far-off and exotic land, i.e., England, he asked: "Catching owt, lad?"

Earnestly, because, as I mentioned earlier, I was apparently quite a serious kid, I told him I thought I'd had a bite about three weeks previously, but then again it might just have been the hook getting caught on a reed. Without any hint of scorn or impatience, he carefully and meticulously showed me where I was going wrong.

My set-up was the big problem for starters – it gave basic a bad name. Line as thick as telephone cable, bubble float the size of a coffee mug, a hulking great ship's anchor of a hook and bait that consisted of huge worms that could have passed for the younger cousins of anacondas.

"That 'ook's about a Size 8…you want 18 or 20. And lad, you'll find the fish will appreciate a bit of a feed. You want to bring them to you, not waste your time chasing around after them."

A beginner's guide to coarse fishing in a three-sentence nutshell.

He set me up with a trace of gossamer fine line, a delicate quill float, hooks smaller than I knew existed and a tub of maggots. Then he explained how to use them. All the while, he was using a catapult to spray the water to his right with loose feeding, gifting me a swim of my own. I fished half a dozen yards away from him and, to my utter astonishment, actually started catching a few perch and roach.

Thanks to the inspiration of the mystery man – so free with his time, knowledge and bits of kit – the canal began offering up a few rewards. Pocket money was saved, proper coarse fishing gear bought, articles in the angling mags devoured, expert books borrowed from the school library and sometimes not returned. (To my shame, I still have one of them in my bookcase, 50-odd years later.) There were still blanks, of course, but they became fewer and to make up for them, sometimes it was ludicrously and effortlessly easy.

Even when the usual distractions of youth came along – music, non-waterproof clothes, hair, hormones and yes, even a little schoolwork – I kept faith with the fishing. My mates and I even tried specialising a bit, targeting specimen perch and roach rather than just filling up our nets with little ones and, in those distant barbaric days, chucking out a live bait for pike while the smaller fish entertained us as we waited for one of those scary predators.

The canal remained our rock-steady home fixture but we began branching out a bit too. A few bike runs to small rivers to try, mostly unsuccessfully, for trout. The occasional fruitless go for salmon on the Forth, a bus ride away in Stirling. Then we discovered a new fishing haunt and, at the same time, learned how little we actually knew about real life.

First time out, we were three teenage lads going fishing on the dawn and thinking we were it and a bit. Boasting about how we'd con our way into a half fare even though two of the three of us were showing signs of not having shaved for a few days. Cracking up when the oldest looking of us, big Brian, who could already get served in the offy, told the bus conductor with a straight face and a voice like gravel that he was eight.

Five minutes into the journey on the smoky top deck of the 5.30am bus, we were reduced to a kind of squirming, blushing mush. Our bravado had been punctured by the women puffing on freebies from the cigarette factory where they were heading for early shift, winding us up with lurid taunts to amuse themselves. The wicked, raucous cackles shredded our nerves as they squeezed in between us and offered to sit on our knees and play with our rods.

Our brashness had been replaced by relief by the time we got off the bus, forced to admit, though not out loud, that we were innocents at heart, no matter how much we'd imagined we were grown-ups. In fact, it took us a good 20 minutes to turn the story round to our advantage and start bragging about fighting off a bunch of older women, proper Mrs Robinsons in fact, who in reality were probably no more than mid-to-late twenties.

OK, they had messed with our heads and our self-esteem but at least we had the fishing. That's what we had come for and for a while, our new place even relegated the canal to second choice.

This was Hogganfield Loch, where we started going in the early 1970s after seeing an article in the Angler's Mail about *a new top-secret water* in Scotland. Big-name coarse experts had come up from south of the border to file despatches of extraordinary catches of giant roach. It was only when we studied the pictures closely and glimpsed the rhubarb fields in the background – a famous old Glasgow landmark you'll remember if you're anywhere near as old as me – that the penny dropped. That's no top-secret water, it's only Huggie. So began treks on the first morning bus, even if it meant running the gauntlet of the merciless ciggie-factory man-eaters.

Incidentally, as I write this, I begin to wonder if my memory is playing tricks because I seem to recall a sort of hazy smoke emerging from the surface on some of those mornings. My friend Google has just informed me that there is a field of natural gas under the loch which in certain conditions seeps through the clay bed and creates the effect of fog coming out of the water.

The fishing was invariably outstanding. It was the only place in my early fishing days where we sometimes caught so many that we ran out of bait. I remember one time, on a solo trip, having to jump on a Corpy bus and nick into the city centre to buy more maggots from Caffaros, the legendary tackle shop at the top of Renfield Street.

Meantime, the primary problem locating the huge roach was getting past the massive shoals of suicidal perch which infested the margins. I found the answer by accident late one morning when, yet again, the maggots ran out. I couldn't scrape up enough loose change for a bus ride into town, so I tore lumps from the inside of my rolls and discovered the roach couldn't resist the chewy, doughy bits from the middle.

Talking of dough, we once raked in a fair bit of the other kind from a bunch of Japanese tourists, the first we'd ever seen. Hogganfield Loch, it must be said, isn't exactly your wee bit hill and glen type of spot. It's more big urban park pond flanked by grey housing schemes. God knows how it was described in the tour brochure. Charming waterway in the heart of a vibrant city? Enchanting lake amidst exotic gardens? However it had been advertised, the Oriental holidaymakers looked genuinely thrilled to be there.

Smiling and bowing politely, the couple of dozen who had got off the tour bus stopped to see what we were up to. Right on cue, one of our floats dipped and yet another fat roach was on its way to join its mates. Before we knew it, the grinning tourists had formed an orderly queue and were taking souvenir snaps of each other holding up our dripping keepnet which was heaving with wriggling perch and roach. Even better, they were happily paying ten bob a time for the privilege. For anyone who claims they don't know what ten bob means, it's the olden day equivalent of 50p. Taking inflation into account, we were practically millionaires by the time we went home in the hired limo.

What we didn't encounter back then was any bother from the locals. Some years back, when I was contemplating a nostalgic return trip to Hogganfield, I came across shrill warnings screaming out on the internet. One website listing coarse venues claimed that the recommended gear for the water included a good pair of trainers – for making a swift escape! I've since heard of anglers being pestered or threatened and some serious carp specialists told once of being fired at from air rifles. That may well have been tongue in cheek or at least exaggerated but it did bring back unpleasant memories.

I found myself up against a similar peril on what, if memory serves me right, was the final canal expedition of our youth. It was a kind of informal last day's fishing for a mate and me. We'd both just finished school and were heading off in our different directions. I was about to start my first job on a local paper and Martin was going off to London to study map-making though, bizarrely, he returned a few years later flogging Mars Bars and driving a flash company Cortina. (By the time we got back in touch 25 years later, he was running Dyson, the fancy vacuum folk.) So no, not the most glamorous farewell gig but we did have colourful memories of the canal, not least of the day his first ever pike was hastily cooked over a fire and eaten…but more of that later.

We were riffing on daft stuff like that when we were interrupted by a crack and a zing and something zipped into the water in front of us. The accompanying sniggers were quickly traced to three young kids on the far bank, aiming air pistols at my pal's pike float. A couple of strides towards the bridge and a few growls about inserting the guns into orifices not designed for the purpose, were enough to send the wee neds scurrying back to the housing scheme not far from where we were fishing. But not before they vowed to return – *wae a team.*

We'd had a run-in (run-away is probably more accurate) with *a team* in that part of the world once before and discretion is the better part of valour and all that. So, just in case the kiddie gun gang really did return with reinforcements, we headed off to a secluded quarry a mile or so away that we and another bunch of guys had been crudely stocking on and off for a few years with fish carted in buckets from the canal.

Thinking we were safe and out of sight, we fished away happily enough for an hour or so, quite pleased with the results of our non-scientific transplanting of perch and roach…until we found ourselves in the middle of a bad cowboy movie. Until then, I'd never really bought into the old cliché about how you can sometimes feel eyes watching you. In the same moment, we both glanced up at the cliff

33

towering above the quarry on the opposite side. One by one, figures popped up, each waving pistols or rifles and whooping like pesky Injuns, sorry, Native Americans. Never have I packed up fishing gear so quickly – who knows what we left behind – as we were pursued by a mob that in hindsight was probably only seven or eight strong but seemed at the time like a huge, tooled-up posse.

That reminds me of another quarry and another youthful lesson learned, this one about giving up secret fishing spots. As I've explained, where I grew up, if you wanted to go fishing and couldn't afford the bus fare to Huggie, it was either the canal or the canal. Overall, it was a decent enough place where sometimes you'd catch a dozen or even 20 in a session and go home feeling like a hotshot but where you also knew you could easily be skunked. It was reaching the same old same old stage when I first heard whispers about the fabled quarry, just outside Cumbernauld.

What really excited me was that the rumour had come not from another angler but from a friend of my old man who had come across it while roaring around country lanes on a motorbike. He knew I was into angling and told me of seeing what he thought was a massive shoal of fish from high above the disused, flooded pit.

He gave me rough directions and after a couple of abortive scouting missions, I found the place. It might have been well off the beaten track but it was far from a picturesque wilderness. One long side was protected by sheer cliffs hewn from decades of blasting and digging, another was unpleasantly boggy. The only accessible sections of bank were strewn with rubble and jagged chunks of rusting machinery.

FISHING IN THE SUN

OK, not promising, but once I'd picked my way through the debris and created enough space to set up my gear, it became a personal paradise. That first time, I stopped counting at 120 perch and for the only time in my coarse fishing years, I had to empty the keepnet twice and start again. I'd gone after school and had to get home on my bike before dark so even if it was summer, I would only have had four hours tops which meant I was catching at a rate of a fish every two minutes. It was non-stop cast, watch the float dip under, bring in perch, unhook it, drop it into the net...and repeat.

In the next couple of weeks, I saw not one other angler or any telltale sign that my private hotspot had been rumbled. OK, I never caught 120 in a session again but the catches were in the dozens and, even better, the fish were of a decent if not huge average stamp.

Then I killed it for myself. I took my best fishing buddy to the quarry and swore him to secrecy. Then he took his next best pal and swore him to secrecy etc etc. Two Saturdays later, you had to get there by first light just to grab a space.

As a postscript to this memory, a year or two ago I mentioned the mysterious old quarry and its approximate location to my brother, who still lives in the area where we grew up. I clung to the hope that somehow the quarry might have been abandoned, forgotten and gone wild. With romantic notions of revisiting my youth, I wondered if somehow the spot had become a secret all over again, once more teeming with lonely fish waiting to be discovered by me. But Kevin smashed my dream with a simple reply.

"What, you mean The Perchy?"

Then, just to confirm that a return mission to the fabled quarry of my childhood is never going to happen – at least not in its original guise – I did a bit of digging. I discovered it was later transformed into Magiscroft, Scotland's first major fishery dedicated to coarse angling. Oh well, at least it's still got perch in it.

Chapter 3

Fishing's Archie McPherson

NEXT time you're at a trout fishery and every single angler is catching except one poor sod over in the corner, come and say *Hi* because there is a decent chance it will be me. Unless you are Mr Infallible Super Angler, you will have had one of those days. Or maybe even a few, depending on just how many you are willing to admit to.

All around you, rods are bending. The air is ringing with phrases like *ya dancer* and *get in there*, little yelps and grunts of satisfaction and all the other particular, personal noises folk make when they hit a fish. Trout are fighting for all they are worth, burrowing deep then thrashing around on the surface en route to nets. There is a mood of general exuberance on the banks and on the platforms and on the dam walls.

But you can't join in, you are excluded. There are no whoops of joy from you. There is none of that because you are the exception, the odd man out. You cannot buy an offer, never mind a fish. You have been through the fly box, then back through it again. You have ripped lures, you have left dries bobbing in the ripple, you have trailed Diawl Bachs and Crunchers in a slow figure-of-eight. You have attached *Please Bite Me* signs to bugs under an indicator. But nada, nothing, not a sniff. Yup, I don't mind admitting it has happened to me – more than once – and it's not pleasant.

You start to doubt every aspect of what you are doing and imagine that somehow your fly has turned into Houdini and detached itself from your line. It's a lonely experience too because no one wants to speak to you. No one wants to come close in case they catch the bad vibe hanging around you. You are utterly miserable. In fact, it can be one of the worst feelings in…

No, hang on, get a grip, we're talking about fishing here, not the actual serious stuff of life. The thing about a blank is, you'll get over it and anyway, nobody died. Well, maybe your soul, but that doesn't count and even if it does, no one else cares. We'll study this more in depth later.

If it has happened to me, then occasionally, just occasionally mind, it has also worked the other way round. Like the day I sensed that all was not well as soon as I got out of the car at a well-known trout fishery that I've fished a handful of times over the years. I saw grim faces and slumped shoulders, I heard groans and low-pitched mumbles. I heard familiar, bad-day phrases like *totally brutal man*, and *no' a fish in the place.*

The trademark beaming smile of the normally affable fishery manager was absent. His head was down and he was frowning. He had a band of restless natives on his hands – guys who had paid their money and were using up the day's fishing they had been looking forward to all through their working week. They weren't catching, they weren't happy, they wished they'd gone somewhere else and they needed somebody or something to blame.

Not exactly the most promising start to a day's fishing, is it? Especially when you walk into the lodge, or the plain old hut, or the Portakabin, and there's an atmosphere like there's been a death in the family. Your heart sinks because you have spotted a few familiar faces out there and you know they are accomplished anglers, so what chance do you have? Before you even get the rod out of the boot, you know a difficult, perhaps fruitless day is in prospect. If only you had been quicker off the mark, spotted the gloomy faces and executed a swift three-point turn in the car park without catching anyone's eye. You wonder if you could still get away with faking a phone call and blurting out that you've just been called away at short notice.

"It's fishing hard the day," confesses bossman. "Don't understand it. Been brilliant all week as well. Fished its pants off yesterday, so it did. Ask anybody."

For a brief moment, you kick yourself for not phoning first to check the form in advance. Then you give yourself a shake and remember the first, most basic lesson of fishery logic: phoning ahead to ask how a place is fishing is a complete waste of time.

Before I explain that, let me say a few words about fishery owners. I've met plenty of them and they are, in the main, a friendly, honest and enthusiastic bunch. But if you think they're living the dream, then it's a hard dream. Think of all the everyday factors they can't control – weather, competition, weed growth, stocking costs, roadworks, badly behaved fish refusing to bite, social media attacks. Then chuck in the small matter of a global pandemic.

Worth bearing all that in mind before you ring to ask if the trout are in party mood.

Yes, a fishery is a place of leisure and, hopefully, enjoyment. But it is also a place of business. It is someone's livelihood and there is a very simple equation at play. To stay in business, you need customers.

You wouldn't waste your time ringing a restaurant you are planning to eat at and asking how the food is that day, would you? I mean, what are they going to say?

"Well, actually, the steaks are tougher than wading boots, the veg is well past its sell-by date, the last person that had the fish got food poisoning and the ice cream is warm. In fact, if I was you, I'd try that other restaurant across the street."

Not going to happen, is it?

So, using that logic, when someone calls and asks how a place is fishing, what do they expect to be told? Seriously, let's be realistic.

"Look, it's been crap for days, you'd be better spending your money on that rival fishery down the road. I've hardly got any customers left so I can't afford to stock the place. So what if I can't pay my mortgage this month, get my house repossessed, my wife leaves me and my kids think

I'm a dick. All I care about is that you have a good day's fishing. So no, don't come within a mile of this place. You'd have more chance of catching a trout in your toilet."

Can't imagine having that kind of conversation when I phone a fishery to help me make up my mind on where I'm going to spend my leisure time and money. Not that I'm suggesting for a minute that they'd actually tell you lies. No one is daft enough to claim that the fish are fighting each other to get at anglers' flies when they know you'll find out the truth soon enough once you turn up. No, they'll couch it in such a way that would get them off the hook, pardon the pun, if an angler was outraged enough to take them to the small claims court for obtaining money under false pretences. You'll hear fishing conditions described as *a wee bit slow*, or *up and down,* or the real end-of-tether classic, *well, the fish are there to be caught.* Then there's the get out of jail card – *not sure mate, been busy in the hut but I think the boys are doing all right.*

So no, don't waste your time ringing in advance for a check on the fishing. All you can do is go on the experience of your own past visits, word of mouth and the latest chatter on social media from names you trust. And if your visit doesn't live up to expectations, you either blame your own failings or put it down to an uncharacteristic off day at the particular venue. Of course, you do have the option of not going back. There's not exactly a shortage of trout fisheries so there are always alternatives.

There is another side to all this. The side that led to a weary fishery owner once telling me: "You know Mike, running a fishery would be the perfect business and the perfect life…if it wasn't for the bloody anglers."

To be fair, he had just emerged shaking his head and slapping the back of his skull after dealing with a couple of unhappy customers. The first was a guy insisting that when he paid for a four-hour ticket, that should mean four hours of actual fishing and not include time spent tying on a new leader after he was snapped off by *one of your flamin' trout,* or the 20 minutes he'd stopped for lunch. Seriously.

The second moan is apparently more prevalent than I would have believed – a disgruntled bloke asking for his money back because he hadn't caught a fish. Probably the most popular cliché you'll hear among anglers, especially on the slower days, is that our sport is called fishing and not catching. The reason it's a cliché in the first place is that it's true. Sometimes it just doesn't happen and you've got to suck it up, accept that paying for a four-fish ticket is not the same thing as being handed a guarantee that you'll catch four, three, two or even one fish.

Not so long ago I caught a little snatch of conversation that spoke volumes. I'd turned up at a favourite trout fishery of mine for a wee afternoon session as two guys were packing up at the car next to mine.

"Not be back here in a hurry," said the first one.

"I know, pure garbage," his pal chipped in. "He's obviously not bothered his arse stocking the place for months."

Can you imagine two golfers blaming the course or the club secretary because they couldn't find a fairway or sink a putt all day?

The fishery owner was honest enough to tell me immediately that it had been rock hard all day with only the odd trout caught. The unspoken code was, *Look, you haven't paid or tackled up yet so you can still change your mind and go elsewhere.*

I decided I had come a far distance so I might as well give it a go and maybe I just hit it lucky and chanced upon a two-hour window when the fish suspended their awkward sods act, but I had some good sport and saw plenty of life in the water. But it reminded me yet again why I don't envy the guys who run the commercial waters where so many anglers spend their days off. As if to reinforce the point, over the next couple of days I saw two fishery owners moved to defend their stocking levels after unsubstantiated, anonymous allegations on social media.

Now, I get that folk fork out their hard-earned dosh to fish and that entitles them to mump and moan when they don't have a good day. But I like to think that the vast majority of day ticket anglers are philosophical about the days when it doesn't work out and look to themselves first when they don't catch.

Back to where we started, remember? Oh yes, that morning when I got out of the car to a torrent of grumbles and groans. The fishery owner had no option but to play it straight when I asked if there was much being caught. Best he could summon up was: "Well, I think one of the lads dropped one earlier."

Not exactly brimming with confidence, I sauntered round to a spot on the far bank away from the muttering masses, or the disgusted dozen, to be precise. I can't remember exactly what flies I started with, but it would probably have been a pair of standard dries – an F-Fly and a Yellow Owl, something like that. The kind of flies that look like nothing in particular but a little like a lot, if you

43

know what I mean.

When the first fish arrived within four or five casts, I was pleasantly surprised.

"Got to be one daft troot in the place," someone shouted over jovially. A few guys chuckled and I was happy to join in the banter.

"Yup, had to get flukey sometime," I called back in the same spirit.

By the time I'd netted and released my second then third fish within about 20 minutes, the laughter had died. Then came fishery logic lesson No 2. *The trout are all shoaled up in the one spot and that's the only place where you'll catch them.*

The way I had this confirmed was that I took a quick break behind a gorse bush for, you know, the same reason we all take quick breaks behind the gorse bush. So that's what, minute, minute and a half, two minutes tops? Long enough, as it turned out, for my spot to grow a squatter. In my brief absence, one guy had nipped over and was standing next to my rod, already casting. Another bloke was settling in a few yards away with yet a further two starting to wander in the same general direction.

"Aw, sorry mate," said my new neighbour. "Didn't realise you were still fishing here. Don't mind, do you?"

There was stupid old me thinking the rod, the bag and the landing net might just have been a tiny bit of a clue that yes, I was still fishing there. But what the hell, the last thing I go fishing for is to have an argument and who wants to be called a hotspot hogger?

So, anything for a quiet life, I picked up my gear and wandered about 30 yards further along the bank. I'd already had a few fish so I wouldn't have complained if normal service had been resumed and I started struggling with the rest of them. But the fishing fates weren't having it, or maybe the trout had held a committee meeting and voted a plain Size 18 Olive CDC as the one and only fly they would touch that day. Two more fish within five minutes and I could feel a black cloud of bitter resentment drifting towards me from all round the fishery. The stalker back in my old hang-out – actually, two of them by now – looked like they were arranging a mob hit.

Now I'm sorry, I know it was petty, but I couldn't resist. I gave them a wave.

"Guys, why don't you come on over here?" I shouted. "Bags of room."

Hands up, I deserved their response, one hundred per cent.

"Aw, cheers mate," they called, waving back as they started heading along to join me.

If there was one consolation, it's the certain knowledge that a day when I am virtually the only one catching ain't going to come along very often. The other consolation was that though I had already met The Space Invaders, none of the other classic fishery characters seemed to be around that day. We've all met them but look away now if you are easily offended.

THE ARCHIE McPHERSON. Maybe it's just me, but I have this daft notion that peace and quiet are big parts of fishing. After all, it's the section of your life where you leave the stresses and pressures of work and family behind, when you get out of the traffic and the bustle – even if it's only for a few hours at a time.

But someone forgot to tell the fishing version of the football commentator. Nope, he doesn't even consider the tranquillity part. He is the bloke who has somehow got it into his head that you, and every other angler in hearing range, want a running commentary on his fishing. Hearing range, by the way, can mean the opposite bank because he is VERY VERY LOUD.

Angling's Archie McPherson will share every last detail of his day, and I mean *every* detail. What flies he's using. *That's me stickin' oan a Cat's Whisker.* He'll transmit every trout rise. *Did youse all see that? Bastard came up there the moment the flea hit the water?* (Just to explain. He asks that question because he assumes that rather than paying attention to your own flies, you would rather watch his.) Each tiny bit of interest he gets from a fish is relayed. *Wee pu' there, boys.* (Don't worry, that last one isn't him sharing his trip behind the gorse bush, though give it time and he may tell you that too.) He'll inform you about what he's got on his rolls. *Corned beef and broon sauce, ya dancer.* And you'll even hear what he watched on telly last night. *Any o' youse watch that Strictly? Pure pony man.*

Archie is usually easy to spot because he often wears a snazzy hi-viz jacket just in case others don't notice him. Sadly, being able to spot him and avoid him are different things entirely. Taking note of the yellow garb will do nothing to turn down the volume.

THE NEW PAL. Like the Space Invaders we met earlier, the New Pal also lives by the belief that all of the trout in stillwaters – without exception – congregate in the one place. He abides by the rule that if one guy gets a fish, suddenly he needs a fishing buddy. But the New Pal's additional and equally valuable piece of acquired intelligence is that you can only tempt fish with the same fly that the guy next to you is catching on.

Now, let me be clear here. I've had days that have been rescued by the generosity of other anglers who have shared both knowledge and flies. Equally, I am never slow to pass on a fly that is working for me to another guy who might be struggling. That is, of course, if I've got at least three of them on me. I mean, come on, there's generosity then there's blind stupidity.

But the New Pal isn't content with the fly you give him. He also needs to cast directly across your line because in his book it isn't just about which fly the fish will take. It's also about the single, exact spot in the fishery where the trout are waiting to come to that fly. But fair enough, you expect that. What you might not expect is that if he happens to snap off the fly in weeds or on the low branch at his back, or if he is broken by that trout he has so skilfully located directly out in front of you, or even if he has simply dropped the fly in the long grass, then you are duty bound to give him another one. It's like a kind of law. Same applies if you change and catch on a different fly. Once you've established that kind of rapport, willingly or otherwise, you would be the worst kind of rat if you didn't offer one of those to your new pal too.

THE HYPNOTIST. A cousin of the New Pal but more complex because even though he wants your killer fly, he will not lower himself to ask for it. Instead, he will apply mind control powers to force you to offer it to him.

He will materialise in your life when he sees that you are catching steadily while he is not. He concludes that you hold the key to making his day better and that he is capable of supplying sufficient psychological pressure to make that your priority too.

Typically, you will meet the Hypnotist when you are kneeling or crouching to release a fish. Sometimes you will sense a presence close by, perhaps see a shadow that wasn't there a moment ago, or think you can hear faint breathing. When you turn your head, you realise he is standing there, looming over you. If you are unlucky, you will jump in fright and end up feeling a little embarrassed which will immediately give him an edge. As you get up, you become aware that he is standing uncomfortably close. He will usually break the ice by telling you how well you are doing, like a teacher acknowledging a primary school pupil who has just cracked joined-up writing.

He will quiz you on the name of the fly and then ask to see it. He will make a point of taking it from your hand or your box, holding it and studying it closely. He will hand it back, make a tutting sound and say something like: "Aw man, I don't think I've got anything like that in my box. Don't know what I'm going to do. Do you mind showing me it again and I'll see if I can find something remotely similar? If not, I'll go online tonight and buy one for next time."

The whole performance is a waste of time because chances are you would have given him the fly if he had straight-out asked for it – and probably still will anyway. Now you are reluctant and find yourself resisting because you know exactly what his game is. But he is prepared to wait until you crack.

THE PEG HOG. Another fact about fisheries that a lot

of anglers may not be aware of is that when you hand over the cash for your session, it's kind of like taking out a mortgage. It is as if you actually have title deeds to one little piece of bank for the duration. At least, that is what the Peg Hog thinks because he will set up living quarters at his chosen spot. He'll put down little boundaries, using pieces of equipment like his landing net and bag. He'll usually have a collapsible seat with him to make himself comfy and feel at home. If he could, he'd put up a pair of net curtains for privacy and arrange to get his mail forwarded until his day ticket expires.

Nothing makes him budge from Chez Fishing Spot, well, apart from his lunchtime roll on sausage and mug of tea in the fishing hut. But that's not a big problem. He simply leaves his gear spread around along with a homemade sign warning that trespassers will be held face down in the water and drowned. Oh, another thing. I've not actually seen this myself, but I've been reliably informed that the Peg Hog lifts his leg to mark his territory.

And, of course, there's another one of those characters you come across at fisheries that I haven't mentioned yet – the Smart Arse. He's the guy who makes fun of his fellow fishers, like the ones above. Next time you spot the Smart Arse at a fishery, come over and say *Hi*.

Chapter 4

Taken by surprise

WHEN I started an angling column in The Scottish Sun back in 2008, it was a no-brainer that I should concentrate on the most popular type of fishing before gradually branching out. It's a simple equation: you want readers so you home in on what they enjoy doing. A bit of research showed two things. One, fly fishing on small-to-medium commercial waters was the No 1 activity of Scottish anglers. Two, it was an area that wasn't getting a lot of coverage elsewhere.

As a result, I have spent a lot of time travelling around Scottish fisheries over the years, trying them out and recommending the good ones to readers. Among the most memorable places were the ones that took me by surprise.

Here are my reviews of just a few of them from the time.

ALDERNEUK, AUGUST 2012.

I had a score to settle with some trout because on my only previous visit to Alderneuk, I had left with the perverse conclusion that I had never enjoyed a blank so much. The reason I had taken not catching so well is because there is something truly magical about this little fishery nestling among dark woods and farmland less than 15 minutes from the centre of Dumfries. It is a mix of the secluded setting, the hospitality of owners Wullie Colquhoun and Wilma McDermid and, of course, those big beasts which cruise in the crystal-clear water like mirages, often spookily close to the bank.

Which is all very nice and poetic, but at the end of the day a blank's a blank whatever the redeeming factors and, truth be told, the memory of the previous visit still rankled. Yes, I could look back and blame an absolute stinker of a day of relentless, sideways rain and a brutal coldness that chilled the brain as well as the body. I could blame the unfamiliarity of a fishery that I had never been to before, in conditions that were not conducive to reading the water. But most of all, quite rightly, I blamed myself because for all the discomfort and lack of knowledge of the place, the chances did come that day and either the fish got the better of me, or I blew it.

But what was hardest to get my head round was that I had driven out of the tree-lined car park feeling oddly OK about it. No fish, cold to the bone, squirming on the driver's seat in damp clothes and yet upbeat because, and there was no getting away from it, I had simply enjoyed myself.

I think I just plain loved the place and that, allied to the enthusiasm, encouragement and old-fashioned decency of Wullie and Wilma, had made the bitter pill that much easier to swallow. It was a bit like being knocked back for a job you really wanted but the folk interviewing you were so pleasant and let you down so gently that you walked out in a daze, feeling good about yourself.

Still, when I returned to Alderneuk, I sat in the car park for an extra moment and gave myself a stern talking to: *Forget all the nonsense about how much you enjoyed that blank. You've got unfinished business here so get out there, show no mercy and catch some fish.*

Despite the nagging dread that I might be in for a repeat performance, the omens did look promising. First on the water early doors, trout dimpling the surface all around the big tree at the top of the loch, a gentle breeze and good cloud cover.

Happily, it took just 10 minutes to get that previous blank out of my system and the monkey off my back as a rainbow walloped the Yellow Owl I had left to drift. There is nothing that settles the doubts and the nerves like an early fish, the reassurance that even if you don't get another sniff all day, at least you haven't been skunked. A second, bigger, fish soon followed, this one close to 4lb, and I took that as my cue to wander the three-acre, spring-fed lochan in pursuit of the cruisers.

The water clarity here is so good that your day can become about targeting individual trout and the banks are cut so steeply that it always pays to start at the fringes. For fully 20 minutes I tracked one particular fish that studied my fly like it was going to be asked questions about it later.

It circled the Owl, stopped a centimetre away, reversed off, moved back in and started circling again. So fixated did I become on this trout that I didn't spot its pal sneak in and grab the fly from under both our noses.

That set the scene for a day of fantastic fun and it's that level of sport that makes Alderneuk the kind of fishery you must try at least once. And if you blank, the kind of fishery you must try at least twice.

POSTSCRIPT: Customer service is a phrase I don't really like to use about fishing. But the way Wullie and Wilma treat their anglers makes them one of the best double acts in the sport. They have created an atmosphere that is more like a daily social gathering than a business and you don't need to have been fishing there for years before you are made to feel part of the furniture. Of course, this would all be of no use if they didn't have the quality of fishing to match. I would suggest Alderneuk is probably not for the angler whose priority is to rack up a big score, although it might be possible given perfect conditions. It is most definitely a case of quality over quantity and that has only enhanced the fishery's reputation over the years.

LEDCRIEFF, APRIL 2013.

Sometimes, just sometimes mind, everything falls into place. You crack the flies and the method early on then keep belief in them all day. The trout play their part and oblige by biting from start to finish. There is part of me that thinks it would get a bit dull if fishing was this straightforward all the time. But after struggling over a few recent sessions in a seemingly never-ending winter, I reckoned sod it, I was due this one.

The venue was Ledcrieff near Blairgowrie, a new water, well, at least to me. The first bonus was that it scored on location – a delightful woodland loch surrounded by pines, way off the beaten track in the Tayside hills. The second bonus, and a selfish one, was that Ledcrieff was seriously under-fished – at least it was back then – which meant the trout had barely seen a fly for months on the day I picked my way along the bumpy forest track.

With patches of snow still on the slopes behind me and the temperature in low single figures, the fish were lying deep which meant starting with a sink-tip and what I counted on as my fail-safe lure, the WSW. It soon became clear that the fish were on the move, constantly circling the six-acre water. So rather than trying to follow them and risk always being a step behind, I stayed put and waited for them to come back around to me every little while. The result was catching in bursts of two or three then awaiting the next frantic spell.

What also worked was frequently switching fly colour between black and white and varying retrieves. The black version of the WSW was top lure of the day, accounting for about half the fish I netted, but almost as deadly was a White Rabbit with a dash of jungle cock that I'd got from John Mackay over at Morton fishery, in West Lothian, a few weeks earlier.

When the feeble sun appeared occasionally to put the slightest of dents in the chill, I reached for the spare rod with a floater and fish readily came up to a Shipman's Buzzer on the surface or a Kate McLaren an inch or two below.

The rainbows and brownies weren't huge – if Ledcrieff

held monsters they managed to elude me – but these trout hit hard and fought hard for their size and provided excellent sport in a pleasant, peaceful setting.

POSTSCRIPT: I'd been tipped off about Ledcrieff but I was made to wait through that harsh winter for a crack at it. First time it was frozen over, next time the road in through the forest was blocked by snow. But when I finally managed to get there, it lived up to its promise.

Subsequent visits were never quite as spectacular but I had good sport a couple of times, once on dries in a short but action-packed evening session, and another time on Golden Olive Bumbles in bright sunshine.

PARKVIEW, OCTOBER 2016.

I have discovered the Ronseal of trout fisheries. At first glance there was nothing out of the ordinary about Parkview. No stunning scenery, which admittedly I sometimes get a bit too poetic about, and no fancy facilities. What I found though, was plain excellent fishing with resident trout that entertained and impressed with their battling qualities.

In other words, Parkview is a does-what-it-says-on-the-tin kind of fishery. The kind of place where you go for a big dollop of peace and quiet while you try and hook a few fish. Nothing less and nothing much more.

You will get a warm welcome and ready advice – if you want it – on what has been catching before a quick run up to the fly pond where you can park a few steps from your first cast. Then it's on to the well-stocked water with fish in great nick that are not exactly queuing up to be caught but will reward a bit of thought and perseverance.

First good omen on my first visit was that after driving through typically bleak Scottish drizzle, the rain went off the moment I got out of the car at the fishery just a couple of miles from Cupar, Fife. Plenty of trout were making their presence felt, rising and splashing freely, but as it turned out, it was a communal look but don't touch exercise.

Determined as usual to catch on the surface, I went through the box but got only the very occasional sniff of interest. Even my usually reliable, last resort option – a big Sussie Rabbit – got only a few reckless slashes before the trout got wise to it and passed the word round. But you know what it's like. The fussier the fish are, the more determined to crack it you become.

In the end, it was fairly obvious and I'd have kicked myself for not sussing it sooner if I hadn't enjoyed the figuring it out part so much. Turned out they would happily take on the surface but they wanted some exercise first so rather than leaving dries static, I had to make the fish chase. What a difference a bit of movement made, sometimes a slow figure-of-eight across the top, other times a fierce rip through the surface film.

That giant V as the first one took off after my Black Hopper was the essence of why the visual aspect makes fishing dries my first option – and usually my second, third and fourth as well. A mix of Hoppers, biggish black CDCs and Double-Deckers set up a string of testing tussles from then until the action suddenly and inexplicably died in the late afternoon. Possibly they were just gathering their strength for a renewed frenzy at last light but I'd enjoyed plenty of sport by then.

It's unlikely you'll stop and buy postcards on the way

out but if you want down to earth, solid fishing action, then I can thoroughly recommend Parkview.

POSTSCRIPT: Some fisheries grow on you more than others and it's OK to admit it. They're not your children so you are allowed to have favourites. But it took me a long time to put my finger on what I liked so much about Parkview and what drew me back there. You know, there's the water and there's the fish but nothing else that jumps out as particularly special. A few hours and more than a few fish into my second visit, it became clear why the little farmland water had become such a top pick. It's my R&R fishery. Rest and recreation. The kind of venue where you are reminded that you don't have to take fishing too seriously because it's the relaxation part of your life, not your vocation.

Owner Jim Moffat is well aware of that and has mastered the fine line between pointing anglers in the right direction and leaving them with a bit of thinking to do.

On my first visit, they wanted biggish stuff on the surface but it had to be on the move and they turned up their noses if it wasn't. Second time round, they were definitely up for chasing again as long as it was three to six feet down. It also paid to vary the speed of retrieve frequently to stop them getting wise to it. In the first hour, I got a couple and missed a couple on a Green and Black Fluffcat, tied by my pal Alastair Murphy, that is one of my standard go-to lures.

But the action really picked up when I switched to a Leggy Bloodworm in yellow, an unashamed crib from the bloke along the bank who had just marked his birthday with a belter of a brownie to finish his session. I didn't feel too bad about ripping off his method because he had forgotten his phone and I did the honours by taking a pic for him and emailing it later, so I kind of paid him back. His tip was spot-on and the fish just kept on coming to the point where I couldn't tell you exactly how many I caught. In any case, counting didn't seem that important when I was having a bucketload of R&R.

CLOYBANK, JUNE 2018.

I just hope readers of my column appreciate the sacrifices I have made on their behalf over the years. Take one boiling summer's day, for example, when I tussled with an endless stream of willing trout. Do you think I did that for my own enjoyment? No, I did it all for the readers even if I have to confess to being made a little wary about the choice of venue before I started.

When I mentioned to a couple of people that I was thinking of giving Cloybank a go, they made enthusiastic noises and praised the facilities and set-up. But then one of them tempered his tribute by casually mentioning that the place might not be everyone's cup of tea. Huh, talk about damning with faint praise! After a bit more humming and hawing and beating around the bush, the other mutual pal thought he had better warn me that it wouldn't be the biggest water I had ever fished.

But Cloybank was on a list of trout fisheries that I still hadn't got round to writing about for my column and, out of principle, I like to add at least a few notches to my fishing CV every year. Or at least that's how I am able to almost keep a straight face when I tell my better half that I fish so much because it is really work, not pleasure.

I very quickly understood what those two guys were on

about when I got to the fishery, just outside Banknock, Stirlingshire, and the manager, John Penman, took me on a quick tour. Even though I was prepared for it not to be huge, I couldn't help a double take when he pointed out the three dinky ponds glinting in the intense sunshine – probably an acre and a half at most between them.

But you know what, I was there to fish and in the end I had a thoroughly enjoyable time. I think the key was to adopt a positive attitude and accept Cloybank for what it was – a neat, well-maintained little string of waters stocked with fish in seriously good nick. They won't throw themselves on any old fly that you chuck out but once you find the dish of the day, they will feed voraciously and fight gamely.

Despite their small size, the three ponds manage to pack in a decent range of features in miniature. There's the little island in the middle one which the fish hang off, the overhanging tree down the bottom with its natural feeding, the lush top pond where trout were rising most regularly.

For no other logic than it was closest to the car park, I decided to start on the middle pond even though little was showing. For an hour I experimented with a variety of methods and during the occasional scraps of cloud cover, I connected with fish on straight-lined buzzers, dark-coloured lures and Diawl Bachs on a slow figure-of-eight.

But unless you are the fishing equivalent of a very conscientious monk, you can only ignore rising trout for so long. I eventually settled on the top pond where, even in the bright sunshine, the fish were rolling about on the surface languidly, feasting on small flies. The deal soon became apparent. They would take tiny F-Flies or sometimes black

Suspender Buzzers but they didn't want to put in a lot of effort. So it was a case of waiting for the next fish to rise within casting distance then plonking the fly right on its nose and more often than not they would clobber it.

POSTSCRIPT: If your idea of trout fishing is the likes of Loch Leven or the Lake of Menteith or Carron Valley, you wouldn't give Cloybank a second glance. Even if you regularly fish the average-sized stillwaters, you would still be dubious. It is the smallest place I have ever fished for trout by a distance. In fairness, it doesn't claim to be anything it's not because the ponds are just one feature of an outdoor leisure complex, alongside a shooting range, golf academy and pony trekking.

It is difficult to shake off the notion that this is not proper fishing and I have to admit that for a while at least, part of me hoped I wouldn't meet anyone who knew me or recognised my mugshot from the paper. I tried to console myself that as an angling writer, I was genuinely there to check out a fishery, which I was, though I also wondered how long I would have to stay until it wasn't rude to slip away.

Then I gave myself a shake and looked at it another way entirely. No one had forced me to come to Cloybank. I was here with my rod and a couple of boxes of flies and in front of me was water with fish in it. Once I changed my mindset, I had fantastic fun. If you can get over the size matters issue, a few hours of watching trout smashing dries then putting a steep curve in your rod is surely hard to beat – wherever you are fishing.

Chapter 5

Don't tell him, pike

TWO of the moments that most shocked me in all my days of fishing happened 40 years apart and the memories have never left me. They gouged deep and lasting impressions to the point that after each incident, I never thought about fishing quite the same again. Both involved pike.

I believe there is a primal instinct about pike that first infiltrates your brain when you are a youngster taking your first, tentative steps in this fishing game of ours. It's the hint of the unknown and the ancient, the sense of prehistoric throwback, the cold, evil eye, the fierce, unforgiving teeth that to a young mind suggest you are dealing with not so much a fish as the cousin of a croc.

Even once you put your wide-eyed childish impressions behind you, it is an effect that never completely goes away. You can chuck a lot of words at it, this feeling about pike, and they come out equal parts contradictory and accurate. Dread and longing, suspicion and respect, fear and admiration, foe and comrade.

When I started fishing at the canal at about nine-years-old, I tried hard not to think about pike too much, though I knew our paths were destined to cross and that I was only delaying the inevitable. For a good while I was happy enough with the canal's staple diet of small perch and roach with the occasional specimen stripy nudging the pound mark. Even then though, I could never escape the disturbing notion that the pike I'd sometimes spot on clear days, lurking at the edge of weed beds like living shadows, were lying in wait for me rather than the next careless or sickly roach.

Pike, you see, or at least stories about pike, had popped up from time to time to leave indelible marks when I was growing up.

The first time my grandfather took me fishing to the canal, he was straight in about the pike. Old Paddy wasn't for wasting time on anything as trifling as perch or roach. At least, not any longer than it took to catch one he could impale on a treble hook and chuck back out to tempt what he had really come for. I was half hoping, half afraid that he would get one. Naturally, I wanted to see a pike up close – as long as there was an adult there and I didn't have to touch it. But I wasn't sure what they were capable of, even out of the water, and what if he asked me to help get it on to the bank?

The story he had told me on the bus from town to canal hadn't helped – a tale he would repeat many times over the years. He had been sent from his family in Glasgow to live with his grandparents in Ireland, as was fairly common back then. He told me that when he was 10, he caught a pike from the local lough so big and so fierce that he had to wrestle it all the way home, its tail and a "fair old whack" of its writhing body trailing on the ground as it tried to bite his face.

Somewhere around that time, I was given a book titled Stories for Boys as a birthday present. It was full of breathless, thrill-a-minute yarns about spies and cowboys and knights and detectives and jewel thieves. But the one I kept coming back to – and probably read about 50 times – was called Death of a Gangster. It was about a pike that dumped a boy on his backside by grabbing the worm intended for smaller fish and snapping the line after buckling the kid's rod. The gangster of the story then ambushed and ate a fat trout before the roles were reversed and it was subdued in a brutal and bloody duel to the death with an otter.

My vision of this predator as an uncontrollable, bloodthirsty figure of fear was sealed by a visit to the Kelvingrove Museum in Glasgow, where the sight of the fabled and leathery Endrick Pike made my scrotum twitch. For anyone who doesn't know the legend, this was an enormous fish found dead on the shores of Loch Lomond near the mouth of the river in the 1930s. The head was preserved and notable angling figures of the day, like Dick Walker and Fred Buller, speculated it could have weighed as much as 70lb, probably more substantial than I was when I first saw it in the museum.

So no, it wasn't difficult for a boy with a vivid imagination to find his dreams – nightmares more like – populated with monstrous fish capable of equally monstrous deeds. But gradually my curiosity and desire grew to the point where I knew I was going to have to conjure up the necessary courage and go after them.

What helped to make up my mind was seeing pike caught on the canal, most of them by a serious Polish bloke whose grim countenance only melted briefly whenever he wrenched a fish out of the water. Sure, his pike looked exactly as I expected – voracious and vicious – but it was a fish, no more than that, and not the mythical, man-eating beast my fevered mind had invented.

Slowly, my pals and I graduated to throwing out the odd live bait – yes, it was the done thing back then – and most times one of us actually caught a pike and survived the ordeal with fingers and face intact. OK, we were still wary but with a bit of care they were manageable and pike became the bonus prize of our canal expeditions.

Even though this was a very different age, it still feels uncomfortable to mention that the first couple of times we caught pike, we killed them to take home as trophies to parade for our families before getting a row from our mums a couple of days later for stinking out the bin. After that though, we put them back, not so much out of any deeply held conservation principles – the phrase catch and release wasn't yet in our vocabularies – but because we concluded they weren't much use for anything other than combat.

There was one notable exception and here's another

confession that still embarrasses me nearly half a century later. I once ate a pike that had just been caught. Yup, knocked it on the head, gutted it inexpertly, built a fire on the canal bank and forced down blackened, half-raw chunks. In my defence, I had the insatiable appetite of a growing boy who had been on the go since 5am and eaten the last of his cheese rolls six hours earlier.

A pal and I who were canal regulars had taken another boy fishing for the first time and, as so often happens, he had made it look easy and landed a jack of four or five pounds. He was inordinately proud and wanted to take it home to show off to his brother, an experienced angler who had scornfully predicted he would catch nothing first time out. Thinking this fishing lark was dead easy, he had wandered off in search of another pike, leaving the two of us in charge of his gear and his prized catch.

Our bellies groaning, we stared at the fish, then at our box of matches, then at the fish again. *Dinner!* I can honestly say we got no pleasure from the charred but largely uncooked fillets we hacked off and skewered on damp twigs which hissed and crackled in our two-bit fire.

If starvation had driven us to a disgusting, foul-tasting meal, there were no excuses for our final touch, our feeble attempt at comedy. We laid out the head, tail and as much as we could salvage of the backbone for our bereft mate to find, exactly where he had left it.

Mind you, I did pay for our culinary vandalism by being violently ill for two days, to the point where it would have been a relief if my stomach had exploded.

Back to the fishing and though I always deny family accusations that I have an obsessive streak (I've told them a million times I don't), I must admit the early warning signs were there in my youthful fishing days. The moment I knew pike had become my latest fixation was when I first described perch and roach fishing as *catching bait.*

I read every word I could find on pike, saved up and bought second-hand specialist gear, spent hours scouting out places I thought might hold bigger ones. Then came the day of that first big shock I mentioned at the start. Or the night, to be more precise.

Almost everyone defaulted to the towpath side of the canal because it was the most accessible and easiest to fish from. But I was once shown a way across a field to the opposite bank, close to a bay which I assumed had been built to allow barges to turn. There was a huge reed bed, impossible to cast to from the towpath, where I figured – or maybe just hoped – pike would have lain undisturbed to grow huge for years. I fished it hard every weekend for a month or so and was rewarded with a good few fish, some of them a bit larger than the standard 4-5lb jacks but no real beasts. Then one Sunday, I hooked the big one. But that's only half the story.

I'd set out by bike at first light and was fishing for half six. From memory, a couple of specimen perch were the highlights of the day rather than anything special on the pike front. Back then, I had to keep an eye on packing up time because I was 13 or 14 and my folks didn't like me cycling back in the dark, especially with a huge rucksack on my back and a rod gripped across the handlebars. But I pushed it that day and it was already gloomy when I got a run on the pike rod.

Almost immediately, I knew this was different class to

anything I had touched before. It developed into the kind of stand-off where even though you absolutely know it's a fish, your mind does a fair job of convincing you it's the reeds you are tangled up in, or a rusty old anchor your line is wrapped around. Eventually, I began to shift the fish and I could almost feel the bloody-minded stubbornness pulsing down the line. As the light faded, the excitement of catching certainly the biggest fish of my short angling career was tempered with the knowledge that I'd be in huge trouble when I got home. Big pike are not on the anxious mother list of reasonable excuses.

Just when I thought I'd never land the thing, I saw my bright red and white float lifting out of the water through the half-light, so I knew it was very close. I've replayed this whole encounter in my head countless times over the years but there are bits that are not clear. I think, but I cannot be certain, that I got a look at the fish. It was definitely no more than a brief glimpse but the picture that flickers in my head is of a kind of log, at least two feet long. Given that my previous best had been a little under 6lb, this was easily eight or nine, maybe a low double. In the grand pike scheme of things, not a genuine monster but it was to me at the time and still a good fish for the canal.

You'll have gathered by now that I didn't complete the job. It wasn't due to any rookie mistakes on my part or the pike getting the better of me, as all fish are entitled to do. Rather, what brought the battle to an abrupt and shocking end was an incident that hit me like a solid fist and that I have never properly understood to this day.

I was steering the fish towards a flat, grassy inlet where I had landed all the others from the bay, when my eyes were drawn to movement on my right, the opposite direction to where my pike was coming from. There was a high-speed disturbance just below the surface and I immediately thought of those old naval war films where the submarine's deadly torpedo flashes through the waves towards a ship. Bear in mind, it was well into dusk by this time but it was like a trough opening up in the water.

Then there was an almighty splash, a brutal thud and my line went slack. My instant reaction was that if this had happened in daylight, the water would be churned up with blood and guts.

It is impossible to exaggerate the power of that incident. The fact I have almost total recall half a century later of not just losing the fish but the effect it had on me, tells its own story. I remember cycling home in a daze then playing the incident over and over in my head during a restless night.

On a basic level, I couldn't be sure what had actually occurred. My inner jury first leaned towards the verdict that the pike I had hooked, struggling on my line and weakened by the fight, had looked easy meat to an otter. But in all my times fishing the canal, I had never seen one and I couldn't help thinking it was a simplistic, neat solution pinched from my birthday book. But the other contender was almost too outlandish, nightmarish even, to imagine. Yes, I knew pike ate other pike. I had read the text books, not just the fiction. But if my pike really had been somewhere around 9lb, what size must its attacker have been to smash it so hard and take off with it in its stride without a struggle?

No teenager likes owning up to being a fearty. But from the distance of decades, there is no denying I was badly shaken up by what had happened and doubtless the darkness closing in had played a part. More than that, I remember feeling insignificant, as if something much bigger than me had occurred, something wild and raw, and I had no real part in it or even any business being there.

I also recall thinking that if anglers were regarded by some as cruel, we weren't even at the races. An invisible, ferocious, never-ending battle for survival was taking place under the surface of rivers and lochs and canals and sea that we couldn't begin to challenge for casual, mindless savagery.

Not that man doesn't have a good go at matching creatures in the wild for brutality, as my other shocking pike moment testifies.

This was about 10 years ago when I wasn't doing a lot of pike fishing but concentrating on trout and flies and constantly seeking out new places to join them together. I had been told about a water run by a private club who reluctantly issued day permits because, I think, it was part of an agreement with the local authority. What made it especially attractive was that the tip-off had come from the manager of a trout fishery who went there on his day off.

The first downer was meeting one elderly regular in the car park who wasn't shy in letting me know outsiders were there under sufferance while he rhymed off a long list of club rules which, if memory serves me right, included length of waders permitted. I like to think I'm responsible and respectful enough not to need a lecture but I wasn't going to let it ruin my day before I even started, so I nodded and carried on tackling up.

I liked the place. It was in a pleasant, out-of-the-way setting, obviously well-tended, with plenty of room to stretch out and roam. I could see various rocky points and reedy bays farther on that I was looking forward to getting round to.

I started off at a bend that had looked like a sharp corner from a distance and within about five minutes, I had caught, and mostly managed to shake off, half a dozen small perch on a Kate McLaren. No problem, I'd move on, try somewhere else, change fly if the same happened again.

My old pal from the car park had started wandering along the bank and when he caught up with me, he asked if it was perch he had seen me catching and returning. When I nodded and casually muttered *nuisances* or *pests* or some such, his expression turned grave and he said: "Bloody right. Just kill them."

I gave a nervous laugh because I couldn't read his face, didn't know if it was meant as dark humour. I mumbled something without much meaning which came out as: "Eh?"

"Club rules," he snapped. "Well, strictly speaking it's just pike but we kill the perch and all. Steal the feeding."

I waited for a second to see if his face would crack and he'd say, *Ah, got you going there.* But no, it seemed he meant it.

"You serious?" I asked. "Killing the pike's part of your rules? The perch as well?"

He misunderstood the look of incredulity on my face and tempered his gruffness a little.

"I know, I know. Some folk don't like chapping them…just chuck them into the bushes."

Let those six words sink in for a few seconds – which was as long as it took for me to hand the guy the permit I'd bought and turn back in the direction of my car.

Just chuck them into the bushes.

I think that is probably the most callous phrase I have ever heard a fellow angler utter. Never mind the killing part, that was bad enough. He was telling me to not even bother wasting my time despatching them quickly, but to toss them over my shoulder and let them gasp their last breaths away. Like the jungle warfare pike attack of my youth, it shook me to the core.

I swear I was determined not to write a preachy book but allow me a brief exception for pike. I don't need to rehash the pillaging they suffer from industrial scale poaching – that's an ongoing battle that needs to be waged. But they can well do without the additional prehistoric anti-pike attitude that still exists among those who should know better.

If you are a roach staring into those lethal rows of teeth, the word *fragile* probably isn't going to be your first adjective for the predator at the top of the food chain. But that is the truth of it and man is at once their biggest threat and their biggest hope.

How many times does it need to be spelled out that pike should be regarded not as a danger or a nuisance to a fishery but as beneficial and even essential? How many facts need to be reeled off to prove their value to the eco-system of a water?

Rather than roaming around *guzzling all our trout*, as you'll sometimes hear, pike target the puny and the weak and the sick and the wounded and the infirm. Like all creatures in the wild, their inbuilt calculator allows them to do an instant assessment of potential grub – the most nutritional value for the least effort and risk.

Here's another fact. They can survive on not much more than their own body weight per year and even when they're piling on the beef, that figure will only go up by two or three times. What's more, they are opportunists so they will eat what is most abundant and that often means their own kind. In other words, kill a big pike and you end up with more little 'uns. So no, a pike cull can never be justified.

As time passed from that day, I started to assume that the club with the pike-killing rule had to be an aberration. More likely, it's what I wanted to believe. But within the last year, I've seen – and written about – a club official showing off his personal best pike while declaring he killed it because it *wasn't welcome* on a private, stocked trout loch. That prompted another angler to tell me that his own local water hosted pike competitions through the winter with every fish killed.

If it all sounds like pike are doomed, then be assured that they also have their champions. In the years I have been writing a fishing column, I have come across no other anglers more protective and respectful of their quarry than pikers, to the point of being almost militant at times.

When I first picked a pike as a Prize Catch winner, they piled in on me, all guns blazing, for naming the venue and thus inviting a stampede. They were right and with the exceptions of Loch Lomond and Loch Awe, which are so vast you're giving nothing away anyway, I've made it a rule not to reveal where pike are caught.

Beyond that, the official organisations and individual anglers constantly preach best practice in catching and handling, as well as fighting the corner of the species with clubs, fisheries and the authorities. It is an appalling dereliction that pike still have no protection in law.

These are creatures of the wild that need to be cherished and cared for. If we have any respect for nature, pike and proper pike anglers must prevail.

Chapter 6

Island flings

WITHOUT having to exchange a word, the two of us edged backwards simultaneously in a feeble attempt to distance ourselves from the impending explosion that was about to vaporise us. The unshaven old geezer held our gaze steadily, grinning at us like a Duelling Banjos extra, his mouth drooping open, exposing the odd, brownish stump.

But it wasn't the gap-tooth grin, or his advanced age, or the fact he obviously hadn't seen a razor for several days that was bothering us. No, it was the two-thirds smoked cigarette balanced precariously on his lower lip, nothing securing it in place, as he poured fuel into our hire car. He had hobbled, bent over, from the tatty little cabin after we pulled into the petrol station and waved his hand dismissively when I reached for the rusting pump. Now he was leaning over the car in a haze of fumes, splashes of petrol spilling as he filled the tank.

We could not unglue our eyes from the inch and a half of glowing ash that looked like it was going to obey gravity any second and fall, possibly straight into the tank. As he took a final deep, hissing, suck on the cigarette, the clear blue skies suddenly turned black which I interpreted as a portent of doom and braced myself for the blast. But instead, violent bolts of rain began battering the ground and bouncing two or three feet back up, like shell bursts in a video game.

The old boy jerked his head and, with a dry spitting motion, propelled what was left of the ciggie halfway across the forecourt. He widened his grin a bit more as he gestured upwards at the newly opened heavens and said: "Faroes sunshine."

Yes, it's fair to say they do things a little differently on this archipelago roughly halfway between the top end of Scotland and Iceland, with a population about the same as Dunfermline or Hamilton – just over 50,000 – scattered over 18 main islands with hundreds of smaller ones in between.

It all takes a bit of getting used to, right from the descent of the prop plane in through a mountain pass so tight you feel the wings must be brushing the sides. (Not that my mate Alan appreciated me pointing that out.) You're barely over that trauma before you're picking up the hire car with the keys left in the ignition because who's going to steal it in a place where no person or vehicle is anonymous? Then comes the claustrophobia of the three-mile sea tunnel from airport to main island, followed by the surprising charm of the houses painted in gaudy yellows, pinks and light blues like a nursery school project.

The surprises and oddities don't stop – grass roofs, live TV bingo with half a sheep as first prize, tinned reindeer, a mindset where anything that swims, flies or has four legs is for killing and eating.

But for all the mind-boggling strangeness taking place amidst dramatic sheer cliffs and plunging fjords, you only need to remember one thing. The fishing is off the scale excellent.

I spent a week there nearly 20 years ago with Alan, who back then was writing a fishing column for a Sunday paper. We were guests of the Faroese tourist board who were trying to promote freshwater fishing on the islands. Sea angling trips around the coasts were already the stuff of legend but it seemed little thought had ever been given to the notion of salmon or trout fishing as a tourist attraction. That, primarily, was what we had come to sample and write about, but it was the quality of the sea fishing from shore that most grabbed our imagination, at least at first.

I had to reach back to my childhood days to find anything I could begin to compare it with. As a youngster, I caught the tail end of the glory days of the Firth of Clyde and the sea lochs of the west coast of Scotland, when big cod and other species were commonplace. I think of my old man coming home from trips out of Ardrossan or Gourock and tipping six or seven double-figure cod into the kitchen sink. I recall the summer night mackerel frenzies on the pier at Arrochar where it was so thick with anglers you risked losing an eye among all the swinging leads and feathers in the fading light.

But even those treasured memories were eclipsed by the Faroes. Mind you, we had to get over a lost-in-translation incident before we could get down to any kind of fishing at all.

Alan and I had a day to kill before our first session on a salmon lake which had been set up by the tourist board, so given that you're never far away from the shore, sea fishing seemed the obvious option. We were looking for a little bit of bait to get us started and after asking around, we were directed to a sea food factory. We asked to buy two herring and paid for them in a currency we hadn't quite got our heads round yet. It did strike us as a little odd when we were told the fish would be brought to our car – until we went back outside to see two one-kilo boxes of herring being carted from the factory on a forklift for loading into our small hatchback.

Our "little bit of bait" hung about like a bad smell – quite literally – all week till I drew the short straw and dragged the boxes from our holiday cottage in the town of Leynar to the communal bins, gagging all the way.

That mishap aside, we couldn't go wrong. It was a simple matter of picking a rock – any rock – or jetty, or harbour wall, and waiting for action. Without a shred of local knowledge, part of the excitement was finding out what species any particular spot would yield.

Sometimes the red cod unique to the islands, sometimes coalfish, sometimes hubcap-sized flounders like the ones under a road bridge across the Atlantic connecting two islands. So good was the fishing and so quickly spoiled did we become, that we once fled a tiny harbour after half an hour because coalies of a decent size – probably averaging a couple of pounds – became a nuisance. Barely had our little silver Mepps hit the water than a shoal would swarm all over them, fish barging each other out of the way to get at the spinners and put a bend in our light rods.

We had an evening boat trip from the island capital of Torshavn where hefty cod and haddock came aboard in numbers. But the absolute sea fishing highlight was a manic afternoon spell on a harbour wall in the port town of Vestmanna where, by some fluke, we hit the tide just right.

This was no scenic idyll but proper industrial docks which added to the surreal atmosphere. Like the rest of the islands, the town and the port were deserted because the Faroes were playing France at home in a World Cup qualifier. For a couple of hours, we were hammered by cod after cod to a backdrop of yells and groans from open windows as those who couldn't get a ticket watched the match on telly in houses or bars. These were serious fish of 6-7-8lb that fought like tigers on our light spinning rods. If we happened to miss a cod on the odd cast, some more of those "nuisance" coalies were waiting to snap up our Flying Cs.

This truly was the stuff of fishing fantasy but we had come to check out the potential of the freshwater sport, a point we had been reminded of when a member of the local angling club suddenly appeared at the harbour where we were sparring with those kamikaze coalies. He shrugged when we asked how he had known where to find us and handed over a bag of prawns as bait for the next day's salmon fishing, a clue in itself to the local attitude towards angling.

FISHING IN THE SUN

If I'm honest, the salmon fishing turned out to be the least satisfying part of the trip. The lake we were taken to was a round bowl of a place where the fish were ending their spawning journeys and it felt a little like they were sitting targets, surrounded by tooled-up locals who plainly were there not for the niceties of our gentle art but to fill their freezers. A gruff old dear with an eyepatch had 13 dead salmon fighting for space in the poly bags around her fishing stool. We found it hard to stomach so we called it a day pretty quickly and headed back to the shore.

The kill-anything-that-moves policy is the hardest thing to get your head round in the Faroes. The first evening we arrived, it was too late to go fishing so we went for a walk to get our bearings and were as puzzled as we were horrified to find a trail of bird wings scattered on the local beach. In the days that followed, virtually every conversation we had with an islander would eventually get round to a story about what species they hunted according to the time of year.

We heard about catching puffins with long-handled nets, the village seal man with the gun licence who would be alerted whenever one was spotted on the shore, the snow hare hunt and, of course, the notorious *grind* (rhymes with wind).

This is when as many able-bodied men and women as possible are alerted to join in the butchering of whales and dolphins – and the sea really does turn red. It is hard not to be judgmental but when you raise it with the Faroese people, they simply and honestly don't see what the fuss is about. Their outlook seems to be that when you live in harsh, unforgiving conditions, and with little labour-intensive industry, you do what you need to do to feed yourself and your family.

After deciding we weren't overly thrilled by the salmon-fishing set-up – and hinting as politely as we could to our hosts that a lot of angling tourists would feel the same about the ritual slaughter – we asked about trout, which elicited a bemused, baffled response. It was almost like, why would you waste your time on those piddling little things when there are salmon and substantial sea fish to be caught? It was so difficult to get past a mindset fixed entirely on the connection between catching, killing and eating.

But we persevered, stressing that trout fishing could be a largely untapped market and eventually we were pointed in the direction of one of the other main islands. I suspected the suggested destination was at least as much to do with the following day being a Sunday because this was one of the corners of the Lutheran-dominated Faroes less strict about observing the Sabbath.

We followed the hastily scribbled directions to a small lake just outside a town not far from the island ferry terminal and were convinced we'd either come to the wrong place or this was some kind of Faroese-style revenge prank because we hadn't been exactly gushing about the salmon fishing.

We had been instructed to park opposite a big steel fence and we would find the water close to the roadside. Our first impression was that we had been led to the town dump. The bank and the shallows closest to the houses were strewn with bicycle frames, bald tyres, half a lawnmower and a section of wall, probably the leftovers from a DIY extension project.

We were on the point of turning back but Alan reckoned

he could see clearer water, maybe 50 or 60 yards further along. Then he thought he spotted a rise. Yes, there it was again. We kept walking and once we were beyond the town – a village really – the water did become clearer and the bank overgrown but at least negotiable.

The trout were not big – 12 ounces was probably the best of the ones we landed – but they were bonny fish with brown and butter-coloured markings and they fought gamely. Most of all though, they were almost pitifully innocent. They threw themselves at Kate McLarens like they were long-lost siblings. It occurred to us that their naivety probably came from being unloved, so far down the pecking order in terms of putting food on the table that neither they nor their habitat were worth taking seriously.

The postscript to that day was another object lesson in the reality of life on a bunch of rocks in one of the most inhospitable outposts of the Atlantic Ocean. After catching a dozen of those little brownies, we ventured a little further inland to a much bigger lake where, we had been told, the fish were not numerous but there was a chance of a serious monster.

I had barely had my first cast when the chilly but calm day was blown away by the most sudden and fiercest storm in which I have ever fished. The horizontal torrent slammed into me like a firing squad on 45mph winds, smashing its way through every barrier I could throw up. The expensive waterproofs ran up the white flag, the layer of thermals was quickly sodden, my bunnet was so wet I felt like my head was in a basin of water. Icy rain was streaming down my back, my teeth were chattering so hard I couldn't form the single swear word (past tense) I needed to describe our current situation. It was early afternoon and I was hungry as well as drenched, so I reached deep into my inside pocket for the cheese rolls that were supposed to keep me going till the return ferry a few hours later, and pulled out a bag of mush.

Alan, further along the bank, shook himself in despair. He looked like someone who had just survived drowning.

Soaked, starving and miserable, what were we going to do? All angling extremists will already know the answer. Yup, we carried on fishing. This was, after all, just more Faroes sunshine.

About 250 miles to the south of the Faroes, and a few years later, it was proper sunshine – and far too much of it – that was occupying our minds as we pondered which loch to waste our afternoon on. I was back on the road with Alan and basking in a freakish heatwave that had me convinced Hebridean was the Gaelic word for Caribbean.

What made it even more unlikely was that back home, the mainland was being deluged by monsoon-level summer storms. So, it was lose-lose – guilt over the families left behind to face the floods while we cursed the truly tropical conditions which were threatening to kill the kind of brown trout fishing the islands are famed for. Temperatures in the high 70s, cloudless skies and barely a puff of wind meant it was hardly worth casting a line until the sun dipped and sensible folk were heading for their beds.

It was my first visit to the Isle of Lewis, but not Alan's. He had a holiday croft with a million-dollar beach view in the hamlet of Gress, about 20 minutes along the winding coast road from the island capital of Stornoway. That was to be our base for the week.

I defy any trout angler to take their first drive across the island and not feel like a kid with their nose pressed up against a toy shop window. *Oh, there's a nice loch. There's another. Oh, look at that one. Got to be trout in there.* It feels like every bend, every rise in the road, produces another water. Big, small, round, long.

Then every so often, you catch a glimpse of the tiniest patch of blue between a couple of mounds in the distance and it dawns on you: all these lochs you are getting so excited about are just the ones you can see. So how many more are there that you can't see? The answer, it turns out, is hundreds upon hundreds.

I heard one stat from a local angler that if you fished a different loch every day, it would take you more than two years to get round them all. That, of course, is if you can locate them and get to them because some lochs are so far into the unpopulated interior of the island – yes, they actually call it *the interior* – that they never see a fly from one decade to the next.

Stop and think about that. Scores and scores of substantial lochs stuffed with trout that are rarely or never disturbed by an angler.

So yes, the weather on that first trip was not conducive to tempting trout – at least not for the first few days – but we had come to fish, so what else were we going to do?

We slogged our way round Loch na Craiobhe, my introduction to Hebridean angling which taught me two hard lessons. No 1: A water requiring a hike of several miles across rough moor, laden with gear and grub in a backpack, still qualifies as roadside in Lewis because, well, you can see it from the road, can't you? No 2: Hebridean midges have more teeth than a pike and thrive on industrial-strength repellent and the angler's usual summer evening pal, Avon Skin-So-Soft.

At the height of the day, with the sun screaming down, na Craiobhe gave up only a couple of fingerling trout but the consolation came in the tiny burn linking it with the next loch in the chain. No wider than a ditch, the trick here was to flick a Bibio downstream on to the moss on the other side, give it a tug and let it plop into the shade of the bank. The near-black trout that attacked it – there is no other way off putting it – scrapped like feral thugs.

Next up was Loch Achmore, where we baked on a boat all day for the sake of an explosive ten minutes when three trout ambushed my Blue Zulu in quick succession.

By the middle of the week, the heat was at its most intense and it was becoming increasingly difficult to rouse ourselves for another day of flogging a loch for scant reward. But sometimes, just when you're ready to write off a hopeless fishing session, along comes the surprise bonus, as I discovered on Loch Ereray, a shallow, low-lying water on the island's north-west coast.

You will be hard-pushed to find a spot more spectacular to fish from than the narrow, shingle ridge which separates the small loch from the crashing waves of the Atlantic. An islander who stopped for a chat as I was tackling up, nodded out to sea and said: "Next stop, Newfoundland."

I couldn't help wondering if it would at least be cooler in Newfoundland. As I went through another round of sun broiling the back of my neck, it seemed the trout, at any rate, had organised a mass evacuation to escape the heat. A long, sweltering hour or two slipped by with the only sign of life pockets of micro trout that were at first a diversion but very quickly a nuisance.

Then the unexpected happened. My Size 12 Ombudsman stopped with the kind of thud that normally signals weed or a boulder. But boulders don't take off for the depths, pirouette on the surface or sparkle silver in the reflected sunlight. After more bucking and charging, a lovely, lively sea trout of a couple of pounds came to the net. Not a big fish by any means but it didn't half rescue my afternoon.

Thankfully, we got two days of more traditional Hebridean weather – overcast, damp and breezy – to save the week with some fantastic sport, particularly on the Ullavats, a pair of small moorland lochs where it seemed the trout were either long, thin and skittery, or deep-bodied and solid, with nothing in between. Either way, they fizzed at the fly and whipped your line in wide arcs as they took off in panic mode.

Nothing will ever quite match that first taste of the Hebrides – the boundless joy at seeing all those lochs, the sheer wild animal abandon with which the native trout fight, the warmth and natural gift for storytelling of the islanders, once you get past what you first take for standoffishness before you realise it's actually old-fashioned good manners. Their demeanour may seem gentle and slow-paced, even a little wary, but underestimate the Lewis folk at your peril.

I've gone back to fish their waters many times over the years and even without that first-time wonder, there are always moments you will store up and treasure forever. Like driving off the ferry ramp at ten to nine at night, being afloat on the smaller of the Ullavats by half past, and catching trout till gone midnight when the sun dips under the horizon to the north-west and rises again shortly afterwards.

Each new trip brings that wake-up call when the first trout hits your fly and it feels like being mugged by Billy Whizz. A sudden whack, the culprit is gone like poo off a spade and it feels like first day back in school after a year out. You need to crank up your concentration levels and retune your fishing to the speed of these brownies. But once you get into the groove, the reward is some of the finest trout fishing in Scotland.

I've encountered trout that hammered my flies deep below the surface in glaring sunlight, others that crashed through the waves when the wind got up in a bid to drown their prey.

With so many lochs to choose from, the fishing here can be as convenient or as far flung as you choose. One morning, I drove five minutes from Stornoway to hit fish on every drift across the breezy bowl of Loch Breugach.

Come the afternoon, Alan and I borrowed a quad and picked our way miles across the vast, desolate expanse of Barvas moor. OK, so we got bogged down a few times and I once tumbled off the back on to, thankfully, a soft landing, throwing my fly rod well clear to protect the important stuff.

But it was worth it for a taste of remote and stunning Loch Mhor Sandavat, where the fish played hard to get. When a couple of beautiful sand-coloured trout with the turquoise tinge finally took an Ombudsman or a Silver Dabbler, it truly felt like a connection with the wild, which pretty much sums up a trip to the Hebrides.

After our usual Chinese takeaway pit stop, we decided

to head for my personal favourite, Loch Roinavat on the west coast, hoping to catch the spectacular evening rise we'd seen before. Or perhaps we'd check out the loch around the next bend instead.

Chapter 7

Mind games

I'VE got a fish on and it's not showing any inclination to slow down, never mind stop, so for the moment there's nothing I can do but hang on. After the initial hit to wake it up and remind it there really is no such thing as a free lunch, it's now firmly in charge and ripping off line for fun.

The skipper, despite the long experience that ensures he's seen it all before, seems genuinely excited. He is muttering things like *wow, that's a fish,* and *enjoy every minute of this, Mike.* He is warning me to settle in for the long haul because this battle is still in the very early skirmish stage and will not be settled anytime soon. In all my years of fishing, I have never been attached to anything like this for raw power. The adrenaline is kicking in and I'm starting to believe that this might well be, to quote the overused phrase, the fish of a lifetime. Any lingering pre-match doubts about my dodgy old heart being up for a fight like this are long gone. I'm fired up, bursting with energy. My attitude is, right, bring it on. Even as the fish steps up a gear and cranks on even more pressure, I'm all in, I'm loving it.

Then wham, she's gone. The big momma is off. Just like that. No warning, no rhyme or reason, no second chances. Everything has gone slack and I'm holding on to nothing. I feel sick. Cheated and sick. An uneasy, crushing silence sucks the life out of the boat and suddenly everyone else is finding something interesting on the floor to look at. The sense of loss is raw and real.

I'm not talking here about the everyday fish that we might drop or the random bites we miss in the normal run of things. That is just part of fishing and mostly we shrug and get on with it. But there are the special fish, the exceptional fish, whose loss is so much harder to get over. I remember a particular salmon as one of a handful over the years that I most regret losing, and I'll get to that in a later chapter. This monster tope was another one.

Every angler will relate to the emptiness and loss I went through that day and how I couldn't stop reliving the episode step by step on the long drive home. The experience itself – and the mental aftermath – made me dig deep into what it means to lose a big one and the broader picture too, the fishing psyche as a whole.

It is very difficult to sustain a career in journalism for

more than 40 years without being a student of people – what motivates them, their ambitions, their hopes, their fears, their needs, how they cope with success, how they cope with failure. Fortunately, we don't need to have a psychology degree or even read the weighty textbooks because angling is the perfect laboratory, the endlessly fascinating study course for trying to figure out what makes folk tick.

Losing a special fish, like I did at the end of a long day at sea, is as good a place as any to start, delving as it does straight into a painful concoction of emotions – helplessness, disbelief, emptiness, isolation – all bubbling to the surface in the two or three seconds when you realise the fish is gone and isn't coming back. Even as you struggle to come to terms with this new reality – the steep crash from high-wire, strength-sapping buzz to effortless desolation – you cannot halt the instant, internal post mortem to figure out if you put on too much pressure too quickly or let the line go slack for that crucial second or failed to spot the kink that fatally weakened the connection.

That is quickly followed by the haunting Back to the Future wish when you would do anything for a flux capacitor to reverse time by 10, 20, 30 seconds to see if you could have done something differently.

Much of the time though, you know it's out of your hands. Maybe the fish wasn't hooked properly and simply let go of the bait, fly or lure. Maybe there's no explanation at all. We all know it happens sometimes without any apparent reason. All those maybes and what-ifs but none of them matter because you will never be sure if it was your mistake or just one of those things.

Of course, you will try to reassure yourself that when all is said and done, it's just a fish and in the great scheme of things it's hardly a tragedy and you just need to get over it. But that won't stop you suffering the regret that you will never really know just how good a fish it was and how much you'd like to have had the opportunity of finding out for yourself.

In the end, you'll have no choice but to try to convince yourself of another reality – that the opportunity has been and gone and there is absolutely nothing you can do about it now, so the only answer is to shrug it off and move on.

What makes this more difficult is the additional element of human nature, the response of the people you are with on the day, because aside from having to deal with the inner angst of losing the fish, you are obliged to immediately put on a front – and without any rehearsal time. You might have a particularly close buddy you will open up to in the confines of the car or over the chippie you always stop for on the journey home. But right there, in the immediate aftermath, in the blokey bantering, you need to grow an extra skin quickly and take the slagging on the chin.

Your fishing pals won't make it easy. Sure, there will be the odd sympathetic noise but they will be lost amid the taunts about bad angling which will be said jokily and without any real malice. All the same, they will niggle at you and a part of you will be unable to stop wondering if they are right. The truth, of course, is that the bravado is something that they themselves are putting on, a secret but collective sigh of relief at the knowledge that it could have been so much worse – it could have been one of them.

You will escape this, the gauntlet of jibes and gags, if

you are fishing alone when the big one gets away but that brings its own set of negatives. Your fellow fishers might pour salt in the wound with their caustic taunts, but at least they are witnesses. In a masochistic way, you need others to verify how close you came and you know yourself how little interest there is in stories of lost fish, no matter how huge, when there is no hard evidence, so you are left to carry the pain alone.

Whether you are on your own or in company, the additional drawback is that the special lost fish are hard to get over and even more difficult to forget because any number of factors will act as reminders for months, maybe years, to come. Fishing in the same place, or for the same species, or with the same mates, or on the same boat, will all act as triggers and, just as you can't stop your tongue probing a tooth with an exposed nerve, it's almost impossible not to mention it and relive the torture.

When all is said and done, losing a special fish is not a matter of life or death. To borrow from the mighty Mr Shankly, it's much more important than that.

The even uglier and more unpleasant cousin of the missed or misplaced monster is the blank, or worse, the series of blanks. The run of miserable, tormented days when the lack of fish gnaws at your soul to the point where you start thinking seriously that yes, maybe you should crawl into the depths of the loft, retrieve the cobwebbed golf clubs and torture yourself on the fairways rather than the riverbank.

Blanking, or getting skunked, or practising your casting, or whatever phrase you use for not catching, feels a bit to me like being eaten alive by midges. You make light of it after the fact, you laugh about it, you boast about the misery of it in a perverse way. You tell self-deprecating stories about how you couldn't catch in a goldfish bowl these days. But it's a protective shield of your own invention because of how miserable it really is when you are going through a barren spell, a misery made worse in direct proportion to the success of others around you.

At some point quite early in your fishing career, someone will have told you, or you will have told yourself, that struggling to catch is part of the learning curve, that blanking is good for the soul, and yes, there is some truth in that. We take comfort from the knowledge that everyone has gone through it. Find me an angler who has never gone through a lean spell and I'll show you someone who is either a fishing god or full of it.

I remember a day on a loch with a guy I fish with once a year. He is a very good angler but he knew he wasn't going to catch before he started. I knew too, because he had told me. I was going to say he had talked himself into a blank before he got out of his car but actually, it was even earlier than that. In his emails in the days before we met up, he told me he was going through a stage where it just wasn't happening. No matter what he did, he couldn't get close to catching. It became a self-fulfilling prophecy.

There were 34 rods on a big loch that day for a not terribly competitive charity competition run by a local angling club. My mate is a club member, an official in fact, and has fished the loch regularly for most of his life. He knows the likely lies and that day he used all his tried and trusted flies while casting his heart out from kick off to final whistle. When it came to the weigh-in, there was only one person who did not register a catch.

I knew what he was going through and it's not pleasant. In fact, if you let it, the experience can become deep and disturbing. The odd blank, of course, is no biggie. When it happens once, it's just your Donald and it's neither here nor there. OK, so you have had a bad day. Big deal, we all have them, go home and forget it. A second fishless day and you're probably still philosophical enough to grin and bear it, though a little bit of you might start looking for reasons, probably to do with the weather or the temperature or sheer bad luck. Blank No 3 and this is when it starts to eat at you.

What am I doing wrong? Did I panic and change flies or bait or lure when I should have been more patient and kept faith in them? Or was I too obstinate and refused to try something different?

If it goes beyond three successive blanks, you are in danger of turning frantic and paranoid. Has my bait dropped off? Are my flies still attached to the leader? But I can't reel in to check because what if a fish is about to bite one of them and it's the only chance I get all day to end the drought?

It nags at you and even more so because you can't share the agony. Well, you can try but other anglers don't really want to hear about it beyond a quick take-the-mick crack. They might put on a front that says it can never happen to them but deep down they are afraid that blanking might be contagious. So they quickly change the subject when you bring it up and if you don't take the hint, they discretely back away from you. Pretty soon, you're the sober guy at the stag night, the misery who brings the atmosphere down, the angling equivalent of a leper.

FISHING IN THE SUN

Even outside of fishing, there is no one to share the burden. You can't tell your family because they have proper things to worry about – the mortgage to pay, the car to get serviced, the sick granny to visit. In the great scheme of things, the fact that a close relative – husband or wife, dad or mum, brother or sister – can't catch a fish to save themselves, is about as important who wins Strictly.

So, you soldier on alone and keep on fishing because that is the only solution. Otherwise, you'll end up in a classic Catch 22 situation (or Catch Zero in your case) because if you don't get out there and work your way through it, you won't be able to tell if you're blanking because you're not fishing or you're not fishing because you're blanking.

Sooner or later, you will work your way through it. The key to making it happen sooner will be to somehow put it out of your mind, to saunter down to the river or loch or shore one day without much thought of fishing in your head at all. You need to get into that zone where you are casting and not caring or at least not fretting and putting pressure on yourself.

OK, getting into that kind of mindset is much easier to say or write down than it is to actually achieve. Ironically, it might help if you have something else to worry about, something on your mind that has nothing to do with fishing. That, admittedly, does go against the grain because arguably the No 1 benefit of angling is to escape into the moment, to reach that place for a few hours or a day where you don't think about anything else, where the past and the future are temporarily irrelevant and you can afford to become completely blinkered, absorbed in the exclusive process of doing one simple thing.

Banishing all other concerns from your mind is not a positive to give up easily but a run of blanks gives you a reasonable excuse. Concentrate on a family issue, or a thorny problem at work, or which Amazon Prime documentary to watch next. Anything really, because the point is not so much to lift the not-catching cloud hanging over you but to forget it exists at all.

When you do crack it, catching fish will feel like the most natural thing in the world again.

There is, though, a way to avoid all that trauma and make sure you never have a blank again. (Well, there are actually two ways but I'm saving my magic method for another chapter.) The one I'm on about here requires a different mindset altogether where you outright refuse to have a blank and, instead, set a simple psychological question that doesn't have a simple answer. *When is catching a fish not catching a fish?*

I got to thinking about this during a joyless day at a trout fishery last year. I say joyless because although there is never, quite rightly, a guarantee of catching fish, it's not a lot of fun when there seems to be hardly any hope. My policy has always been that if I don't catch, the first person I blame is myself. I know the fish are there and if they're playing hard to get, the onus is on me to work a bit harder to solve the puzzle and break the deadlock. Sometimes we have to accept that any fishery, any water in fact, can have an off day. For whatever reason, the fish are just not in the mood, perhaps because of a change in the wind direction, or the light, or because it's too hot or too cold. Any number of reasons.

You need to have at least a fragment of hope though,

don't you? But on the day I'm talking about, there was little encouragement to be found in the shrug from the guy in charge when I arrived around lunchtime and asked how the place was fishing.

What made it even more dispiriting was that apart from barely having a single touch never mind a fish in four hours, I didn't even see one. There were eight others fishing on a smallish water and from all the shrugs and obvious fly-changing, they were all going through a similar slog.

I've never quite figured out if this is a positive or a minus. A positive, because it at least offers the consolation that you're not suffering alone so maybe you're not simply a duffer. A minus, because there are bound to be some good anglers among the others and they will have tried just about everything, so what are the chances of it being any different for me?

As it happened, I got two quick flurries around a Sussie Rabbit on the very first cast without any solid connection. That was my lot.

So, everyone was struggling, no one else seemed to be having any action. Oh, apart from the one guy to my right who, in the space of five minutes, touched two trout, got a brief bend in his rod each time but lost them both. That was the entirety of the activity for the afternoon.

Here's the odd thing though. As that young chap passed me on his way to the loo or for a coffee or whatever, he asked if I'd had any joy so I replied in the negative and, as you do, returned the question.

"I've had five," he said, brightly. "It's usually a lot better than this though – I had 11 the last time I was here."

I took him at face value and was genuinely impressed

97

because it was clearly tough going. I figured I must have turned up late for the party so I asked if he'd got them all in the morning because I hadn't seen a fish caught since I arrived. He looked genuinely puzzled, a little insulted even, and said he'd had two in quick succession.

"Just there the now," he added. "Did you not see me?"

The penny dropped but I didn't argue and just muttered: "Oh, right."

Who was I to burst his bubble? As he walked off, I thought about an argument I'd heard about recently between two competing teams when one lot announced they had been counting fish even if they only touched the leader. I also thought about another angler I bump into occasionally whose policy is that any fish counts if he has it on for a certain number of seconds regardless of the outcome – can't remember exactly how many seconds.

This can't be right, surely? Am I being old-fashioned to think that you have only caught a fish if you actually have it in the net or on the bank or boat?

I am certainly old-fashioned enough to believe that good manners still have a place in our sport which brings me to another classic psychological profile – the split personality, the angler whose behaviour can rotate 180 degrees due to the prospect of catching or not catching.

I can link it to one of the earliest and most basic pieces of career advice I was ever given, which applies as much to fishing as it does to the world of work. It came from my Uncle Matt, a self-made success who started at the bottom and worked his way up in his chosen field. I was 17 and just starting out in newspapers when he told me that the key to success both in and out of the office was to make sure you always treated people well.

The logic was threefold. First and foremost, it's simply the right thing to do. Second, if you ever climb the ladder and find yourself in a position of leadership, colleagues you handle in a fair, decent and human way will be more willing to go the extra mile for you, not just in a crisis, but as a general rule. Third, and most practical, there is a very good chance that the folk you meet on the way up will be the same ones you meet on the way down. Remember the annoying, snotty trainee you couldn't spare the time of day for all those years ago? Unlikely as it may seem when they're damp behind the lugs, never rule out him or her becoming your boss at some point in the future and holding your fate in their hands. Some people have long memories.

How this is also true in angling came home to roost a couple of years back when I arrived at a trout water I had never fished before.

There were two other guys already there, the first a fly-fishing beginner still too demented about his casting to contemplate actually catching. I wasn't much help in that department. My own casting, for better or worse, is self-taught and even though I can usually chuck out a passable line, the last thing I want to do is inflict my bad habits on someone else. Once I'd given him the name and number of a casting instructor pal, John Milne, we chatted for a while and I answered his general questions best I could.

We should all make a point of doing this because who among us didn't have someone who gave us the benefit of their knowledge when we were at that human sponge stage? Remember the way we were ourselves, bursting with questions and eager to soak up every available scrap of information?

The second guy that same day was a regular the fishery owner had pointed out while I was paying for my ticket. I walked past him, said hello, and casually asked what usually worked there in the hope that a little local knowledge might give me a head start. The dour-faced grunt was the first clue and I took the hint when he muttered "different stuff", and turned his back on me. Fair enough, some anglers just want peace and quiet and can't be bothered with the likes of me pestering them, so I left him to it.

I had a difficult but interesting first hour experimenting but started to catch steadily just as soon as I stopped overthinking it and realised there was no complicated secret formula, just little black dries that the trout didn't tire of snaffling.

But my scowling fellow angler wasn't catching and the more I did, the more he scowled. I could hear his disgruntled sighs and mumbles from 50 yards away. After the third, or maybe the fourth, trout in the half hour since I'd started catching, came a dramatic transformation worthy of Clark Kent. Now he was casually sauntering in my direction, all smiles.

"What you getting them on, bud?"

When I told him, he added: "Couldnae spare one, could you?"

Ah, so now you want to be pals? You wouldn't give me the time of day a wee while ago but all of a sudden we're best mates? I have to confess, if my dear departed uncle's advice wasn't still imprinted on my brain after all these years, I'd have been tempted to shrug and say: "Ach, you know, different stuff."

Chapter 8

Nipping down the local

I T is by luck rather than design that I am spoiled for choice when it comes to places to fish close to home. When I moved to the west coast of Scotland 30 years ago, I was working shifts and my children were young so, like a lot of young dads I suppose, I didn't have too much time for fishing, though it was always in the back of my head that I would get back to it at some point. Then I went through my golf phase which was definitely more of a social thing than due to any natural talent because no one ever called me Seve or Tiger without heavy sarcasm.

So, it wasn't until the late 1990s that I looked up and wondered, right, where can I catch some trout around here?

The immediate answer was, well, right here, at the bottom of the garden, because there's a burn running along our back lane with game baby brownies that put a decent little bend in first, a 5ft spinning rod with a single maggot, then a flimsy fly rod I still keep permanently set up with a Size 16 Spider at the back of the shed.

It's when I go a little further than the garden stream that I find the really good stuff – three local angling association waters and four trout fisheries, all within an easy drive. I know Scotland generally has more than its fair share of fish-holding water, but my locality really is something of a trout paradise. Here are the notes I made after just a few of the numerous times I've gone out playing at local fisheries over the years.

NEW HAYLIE, JULY 2019.

It took me exactly one minute to fall in love with fly fishing again. In fact, it was less than 10 seconds from my opening cast before the first trout lunged at the Yellow Owl and reminded me that I hadn't got my eye in yet. Second cast and bang on the 60-second mark, came that moment of connection that has always been the ultimate angling high for me.

I'd spotted the trout rising near the reeds across from the cabin, made an educated guess at its direction, plopped the fly 10 feet ahead of it and, as if on command, it came up for the dry. Sharp flick of the rod, lift into it and it was game on. Cue a fight that lasted only a few minutes but was brutal enough to make the outcome uncertain until the rainbow of around 4lb slid into the net. Quickly, it was unhooked and carefully sent on its way as my heart rate eased back to normal. I was back in the game.

Due to a series of unfortunate family circumstances, I had hardly wet a line all that year but only a minute into the comeback and already it was, oh yes, now I remember what all the fuss is about.

Not that I could easily shrug off the frustration of those months when it was difficult to get out. The winter wasn't even so foul that I could tell myself I probably wouldn't have gone fishing anyway, then the spring came and I could only watch as the days lengthened and brown trout opening day came and went. Worst of all, the frustration of being stuck in through the return of the light nights which I regard as the peak fishing time of the year.

But finally, it felt like I was able to tick all of those boxes they talk about on TV crime shows – means, motive and opportunity. The means were always there, of course, kicking about in the shed. So was the motive. But now I had the opportunity, so it was off for an evening session at New Haylie, in Ayrshire, the perfect comeback venue because it's a water where you can catch on dries all year round. A muggy, overcast summer's evening with a gentle breeze? Yup, no-brainer. Very quickly, it felt like I'd never been away as the trout kept on coming – and that was BEFORE it really switched on and the fish went berserk around half-nine.

My choice of venue after that enforced break from fishing was no accident because there are certain waters where we turn up and it kind of feels like we've come home. Sure, I love the discovery and adventure of the new but there's also the instinct to touch base every so often and in my case that feeling of belonging is split between two venues. One is my local club's main water, both for the comforting, homely vibe and the excellent brown trout fishing. The other is where I get that familiar good feeling when I make the sharp left off the main road and scoot up the little winding lane – New Haylie.

There are, of course, plenty of trout venues around the country where the fishing is terrific but there is something special about this place, an indefinable extra that sets it apart and, naturally, the quality of the sport plays a huge part in it.

We all know that any water in the land can go off at times, the kind of spell where the fish go into a mass sulk and refuse to play. Days like that are rare at New Haylie. It is remarkably consistent with a higher than average ratio of occasions when you will do no wrong and catch from start to finish.

Take one evening visit the year before when the trout fixated on a tiny olive CDC and there was barely a cast without at least a sniff around the fly.

It might be something to do with the rugged, surrounding hills, or the couple of burns that trickle into the five-acre dam, but the fish don't take long to shrug off their stockie roots. The result is that more often than not it's wee stuff, naturals if you like, that will tempt them.

A few years back, for no real reason, I set myself a target of catching on dries in every month from January to December and when it got difficult, I always knew where the best bet would be, but whatever your method, these trout will make you work and fight before you get them in the net.

To sum up then, you've got first-class sport, well-maintained surroundings and an atmosphere where anglers are made to feel more like guests than paying customers by owners George and Senga Murray. What more could you ask for?

POSTSCRIPT: You know those meaningless questions you used to get on the early internet fishing forums, like what if you were allowed to use only one fly for a whole season? It is never going to happen, obviously, but if I was told I could only fish one place for the rest of my life, I would probably choose New Haylie.

I've caught more trout and had consistently better days there than anywhere else and on those very rare occasions when it doesn't work out, the breathtaking view of the Clyde estuary – where you feel you could reach out and touch Cumbrae, Arran and even the distant Mull of Kintyre on the clearest days – comes very close to wiping out the pain.

MIDDLETON, JUNE 2020.

Funny how a day's fishing can be completely turned around right at the death. I suppose it's the equivalent of the dramatic injury time winner after an amazing piece of skill in a football match, or the perfect chip to the green from rough and the putt rolled in from 14 feet on the 18th hole. Even if the rest of the round – or match, or fishing session – hasn't been anything to write home about, it's the special moment that will stick with you and make it all worthwhile.

That was my conclusion after a session at Middleton where I never really cracked the key but still went home on a high.

The conditions had looked pretty much spot on for a

summer's afternoon of dry-fly fishing. Nice ripple, pleasantly cool after a sticky muggy spell but warm enough for insect life to be active. Good cloud cover, no glaring sun, a quick burst of smirry rain that had come and gone in less than a minute. All good, except no one had bothered to tell the fish and they seemed to have decided they weren't having it.

I saw the odd one caught but another angler I spoke to agreed with my conclusion that it felt an awful lot harder than it should have been. But that's fishing and sometimes you've just got to suck it up, dig in, try a bit harder and the trout will either come or they won't.

I've fished Middleton often enough over the years to know it is one of the most reliably productive fisheries in Scotland, so the odd tough one is no big deal. Like everywhere else, it can have difficult days and on this occasion I blamed an awkward sod of a wind that couldn't make up its mind which way to blow. As we've all found from time to time, if conditions are unsettled, the fish often are too.

Not that it was completely devoid of action – a couple of trout came up for unconvincing nudges at first a Yellow Owl then a Bob's Bits down in the bottom corner. Finally, I got one on a Grunter then another on a Harry Potter but the number of fly changes tells its own story – there was no obvious pattern that you could latch on to. I was on the point of writing it off as an uninspiring afternoon and it was almost closing time anyway, when I saw double, quite literally.

Last cast, and the two black CDCs I had on – Size 14 and Size 16 – disappeared simultaneously in violent splashes and suddenly I was fighting on two fronts. A pair of good-sized, solid rainbows battled and bucked and, naturally, wanted to run in opposite directions. Now, the Middleton trout have a reputation for being superb scrappers at the best of times so taking on a pair of them is twice the challenge and twice the fun. I had mentally accepted I'd be happy to land one but after the first was in the net, its partner in crime came surprisingly quietly and was handlined in to join its buddy.

Suddenly the hours of frustration melted away in a rewarding adrenaline rush and I was reminded yet again what a baffling and magical sport this can be.

POSTSCRIPT: As trout fisheries go, Middleton ticks an awful lot of boxes – quality of fishing, a friendly, helpful bloke in charge, peaceful country setting. In other words, nothing the least bit offensive about the place. All of which makes it hard to explain why it has persistently suffered from negative rumours.

A handful of times over the years, folk have told me the place has shut down, it's no longer being stocked, the water is choked with weeds, the manager has been sacked after falling out with the owner or the fish are swimming about with a head at each end. OK, I made up the last one but it has as much substance as the other stories. It is to the credit of owner Paul Allan that he has stuck with it despite all the nonsense.

I have fished Middleton regularly over the years and I have had many more good days than bad. A random entry in my fishing diary for 2009 tells of a bitterly cold morning in November when, like most others, I was plumbing the depths with a sink-tip line without success. Acting on no more than a hunch, I dragged a small Damsel across the surface and immediately got a follow. So I switched to a floater and the trout started playing and didn't stop. I can also testify that the trout are enthusiastic and hard-fighting, with the blues packing an extra punch – a real Middleton trademark. So yes, it is a remarkably good place to fish, especially considering it is not even open. Allegedly.

GLENBURN, APRIL 2010.
Suddenly the wind dropped and the whole place came alive. Already, the sinking sun was painting orange streaks across the sky but it was milder now than 10 minutes earlier. In a far corner of the water, birds started spreading the word in the fading light as out of nowhere, a host of insects threw an impromptu party. The trout decided they were invited too and rose from the cold depths to slurp on the surface. It was a magical moment that felt like the birth of a new season.

How appropriate then, that I was fishing at an old favourite of mine, Fairlie Moor, when I witnessed that moment. Now rechristened Glenburn Trout Fishery, the place had undergone a kind of rebirth too. The previous time I'd popped in for a look, a year or two earlier, it was forlorn and rundown, a little on the shabby side. Now brothers Steve and Tam Maxwell had taken over and were well on the way to restoring it to its former glory. Like me, the pair had happy memories of fishing there and I was certain their sheer enthusiasm would rub off on anglers.

It's the rugged, moorland location that sets nine-acre Fairlie Moor apart. (Sorry, I've quite never got used to calling it Glenburn.) You feel like you are fishing in a remote wild loch rather than a dam just a few minutes off the A78, the main road along the west coast. It's the kind of place where top-quality stocked trout quickly turn as hardy and feral as the setting.

I found that out for myself as I slugged it out with nine of them in a couple of hours, including a 7lb tearaway that leapt on to the bank then back into the water when it realised its error. I also have to confess to an amateur 20 minutes when I was clattered by a string of fish and caught not one. Belatedly, I checked the Black and Green Fritz that had been doing the tempting and discovered the hook had broken off at the bend.

Still, it offered me the perfect excuse to switch to dries as the trout came up to dance into the darkness.

May 2016.

Fast forward six years to one of those days when fishing is so much fun you wonder why you ever do anything else. There I was, perched on a handy tree stump in the pleasant warmth, with a gentle breeze ruffling the water. Jets played etch-a-sketch in the clear blue sky and apart from a dad and son bait fishing on the far side, the whole water was mine. In front of me, soft moorland climbed to the horizon. At my back, the crystal blue of the Firth of Clyde as far as I could see. The trout were rising lazily, mostly beyond casting distance, but I was content to wait for the odd brave one to venture within range.

On a regular enough basis, a fish would either slash aggressively at the Bob's Bit on the point or gently suck down the pale blue Buzzer dangling below the surface on a long dropper. I missed a few, the first due to plain bad angling – stepping on my own fly line – and the second

110

simply one of those mysteries that happens to every angler and is never solved. The third was enough to send an expletive ripping across the water, shattering the peaceful silence.

Time to apply another level of concentration and soon my success rate started to increase, just as it should. From then on, the trout came steadily to the net, regularly enough to keep me interested but not so often that it became monotonous. All gave a good account of themselves, particularly the 2lb brownie which was the highlight among a string of nice rainbows.

A day's fishing which couldn't get much better, eh? Well, actually it could…because of where I was. I'd been deeply disappointed a month or two earlier when I heard Glenburn was shutting for good. Those brothers I mentioned previously, Steve and Tam Maxwell, had called it a day. It was a real shame because they were proper fishing folk who knew the water inside out and ran the place extremely well. As one of my favourite spots for its location and the quality of dry-fly sport, I counted it as a major loss on my list of go-to places.

Then, to my surprise, I heard it was up and running again under the care of gamekeeper Wully Kirk. It might be his first fishery, but he has been casting a rod practically since he could walk and knows his stuff about both angling in particular and wildlife in general. There was talk the dam was to become part of a hydro system but Willy had been assured the water level would not be allowed to drop by more than a couple of feet which shouldn't adversely affect the quality of fishing.

As it stands, Glenburn is well stocked, the trout are up

and at 'em and it's simply a fine place to spend a day. What are you waiting for?

POSTSCRIPT: The phrase feelgood factor could easily have been coined with Glenburn in mind. The good vibes set in and the cares and stresses drift away even as you climb high into the moor before cutting across the track to a water you could quite easily believe was a natural loch until the dam wall gives the game away.

You know how you often hear people saying they are just happy to be out fishing and don't care if they catch? Usually I don't believe them but I've felt that way on occasions at Glenburn. It is a place I have been drawn to many times when I just needed a break. When I first started writing about angling in The Scottish Sun back in 2008, I would dash around fisheries to show my face and try to get the column established. Whenever it reached the point that angling felt more like work than pleasure, I'd head for Glenburn – or Fairlie Moor as I have never stopped calling it. It is my place of refuge.

SKELMORLIE, MAY 2018.

There are some trout waters you take to right away while others grow on you gradually. I very quickly added the newly reopened Skelmorlie fishery to the love at first sight category. Catching a trout on the very first cast didn't do any harm, of course, instantly wiping out the blank risk that can accompany fishing in unknown waters.

But that was just one of the reasons why I was certain that Skelmorlie would join my regular fisheries list. It's one of those places with that hard-to-define positive feeling from the moment you step out of the car – a mixture of no-pressure relaxation and the confidence that you might just be in for some good sport.

It also offers the chance to sample a little bit of angling history because Skelmorlie was one of Scotland's original put-and-take trout fisheries 30-odd years ago before sadly falling into disuse.

It has now been revived with the hugely enthusiastic John Adams at the helm and even though there is still work required to restore the place to its former glory, it's already starting to look the part. I never fished the neat, two-and-half-acre venue in its previous life but a string of experienced anglers have told me they remember it fondly as a dry-fly water of no small repute.

I was able to confirm that for myself just seconds after the first cast to a fish that I'd crept up on after spotting it rising a few times while I first parked, then tackled up. My Suspender Buzzer vanished in a violent explosion and the rainbow fought as ferociously as an over-wintered fish should before sparkling like a bar of chrome when I finally got it into the net.

Any misconception that these trout were going to be pushovers was soon dispelled though. Sure, I caught steadily all day but it was nothing like a fish a chuck and it took regular switching of flies and tactics to keep them interested.

It is true that on a small water like this, the fish have nowhere to hide. But that applies equally to the angler, especially when there is next to no cover on the banks, so stealth and a willingness to experiment are crucial. Over the course of the day, I must have tried and caught on CDCs, Suspender Buzzers, straight-lined Buzzers, Shipman's and

Yellow Owls, and I know John hit a couple on lures when he came out for a cast.

So, first and foremost, Skelmorlie offers good sport from its location high above the Clyde coast, with a view that is a welcome consolation in the quieter moments.

Oh, and then there's the out of the ordinary element that made me pause from fishing for a few moments every now and again. There are, of course, several reasons why you might find yourself delaying the odd cast, like watching for the next rise or waiting for a window of calm in a wind. But holding back so you don't put a guy off his tee shot? That is a new one on me, or did I forget to mention the small detail that the fishery is slap bang in the middle of golf course?

Not that it's a problem as the two sports thrive happily side by side. They might have clubs while we've got rods, but at the end of the day we're all just overgrown kids out playing.

POSTSCRIPT: I've been back to Skelmorlie twice since to check on progress, partly because the fishing itself is so good but also because John's work ethic and enthusiasm mean I really want to see him succeed. About a year after my initial visit, I had a brief session which happened to come 24 hours after a crazy spree on a brown trout loch where the fish had been flinging themselves on flies almost non-stop. I mention that only because my Skelmorlie return turned out to be the exact opposite and I managed just one blue on an awkward night of brassy light and a harsh, chill wind. But the fact I had to work really hard for a single fish made it feel every bit as rewarding as the feast of the night before.

My most recent visit was not long after fishing got the go ahead as lockdown restrictions were eased and I was doing my best to stick to the five-mile limit. (OK, I confess, I broke it by 0.6 of a mile to get to Skelmorlie.) Once again, there was that indefinable factor of feeling good there. John's improvements were plain to see – smart new platforms down one side, the car park expanding, the whole place looking generally sharper.

But forget the cosmetics because once again, the dry-fly sport was immense, even if it meant a trade-off. I'd got a couple of fish early on by targeting risers rather than casting dries blind, but I spotted that the real activity was down the bottom end. And yes, the fish went mad for Yellow Owls but I got destroyed by sabre-toothed midges coming off the firs in the process. Just about worth it at the fishery on the fairway.

Chapter 9

Silly fakers

H IS face broke into a grin and he grunted "Yesss!" to accompany the fist-pump. He and the four others huddled round the old-fashioned grocer's shop scales watched intently as the dial was yanked round, almost to the limit. Nearly off the scale, as the saying goes. There were only a couple of stragglers left to drop their catch into the big silver dish so the cup and the cash prize were surely his. No one else would get close to matching the bumper bag bulging with fat rainbow trout.

The official in charge of the weigh-in, secretary of the club running the open competition on their main loch, stared carefully at the scales then into the Safeway bag holding the fish. Just to be extra sure, he peered into the carrier again. Yes, he could definitely see the pinkish lines running along their flanks. His expression slowly turned from grim concentration to mild amusement.

"Aye, you're not just an amazing fisherman, son," he said to the guy waiting in keen anticipation to be crowned champion. "You're a f*****g magician. The loch's brown trout only."

As the years have passed – *Safeway* was the clue to how long ago the story was told to me – I have become more and more convinced that it is an urban myth. I have now been regaled with this tale of extreme cheating on two occasions, both times with different names and different places. The second time, it was carp and roach instead of bows and brownies.

The first time I heard it, the person named as the villain of the piece was a fly fisher who, for a time, was well known on the competition circuit in Scotland. He also happens to be a bloody good angler, the kind who is capable of making it look ridiculously easy on the difficult days while many around him struggle. I've heard it said of him that he could catch fish in a puddle in the street. I have also seen him in action at close quarters a couple of times and can confirm his skill level. He is one of the best anglers I've ever come across.

All of which makes it harder to believe he would feel the need to give himself that kind of edge in a local club competition…and without doing his homework first. Perhaps the story says more about his accusers. The point though, is that cheating, allegations of cheating and mythical tales about cheating, have been around for as long as fishing itself.

MIKE KERNAN

If you don't believe me, join me on a trip back to Ancient Egypt. I was in first year at secondary when my ears pricked up during a Classical Studies lesson on Cleopatra, the queen known for, among other things, having a fling with Roman general Mark Antony while he was hitched to someone else. Readers of a certain vintage will know the couple better as Elizabeth Taylor and Richard Burton. Cleo was always looking for ways to amuse her boyfriend, like joining him for booze and gambling sessions or wandering the streets in disguise together playing an early incarnation of chap-door-runaway.

One time, just for a change, she invited him on a fishing trip on the Nile. But while everyone else was bagging up on the river's extraordinary perch – which can grow up to 300lb and six feet long – poor old Mark got skunked. Not a touch did he have all day.

But being such a high-ranking military dude, he couldn't just laugh off the blank like the rest of us. It wounded and humiliated him so profoundly that the next day, he secretly paid a gang of trawlermen to dive down with freshly caught fish and attach them to his line. He pulled in fish after fish and as a pile of bright, silvery specimens piled up high on the deck, Cleo and her cohorts were as stunned as they were impressed.

But as any seasoned con artist will tell you, the last thing you do is overplay your hand. You don't show off by catching 20 when 10 is enough. The queen had never seen so many fish landed in such a short space of time. But she wasn't daft and quickly came to the conclusion that the catch rate wasn't just impressive, it was impossible. It didn't take her long to figure out how he was doing it and

118

after a swift investigation, her trusted aides quickly confirmed her suspicions.

She kept her cool though, and made a huge deal of swooning over her lover's achievement. Then she invited everyone back for more when, she declared, he would be sure to show off his fishing skills again.

Back on the water next day, Mark Antony quickly felt a savage tug on his line and began hauling in an obviously good fish. What he eventually swung on to the boat was a big fish all right but it was also clearly dead, gutted, prepared and salted for the dinner table, courtesy of the servants Cleopatra had sent down to pull the same trick back on her boyfriend, only she had taken it a stage further.

Not only was she smart enough to catch him out as a fake, she had also figured out, more than two thousand years ago, the best way to deal with cheats – embarrass them, expose them in front of their fellow fishers.

There could be no more powerful punishment than Cleo's lesson and that is what I can't understand about folk who don't just bend the rules but rip them up. Because cheats get caught. It happens all the time and how do you ever get past it, how do you ever show your face among anglers again? Surely self-respect and reputation are worth a whole lot more than a few quid and your name on a shiny wee trophy.

No, it's too big a price to pay because the result is a stain that will never go away, a shame carried around like a burden for life along with the risk of forever being an easy target for allegations, confirmed or otherwise.

In recent times there was the story of a sea angler taking top prize at a big beach championship down south, only to be stripped of his title because he counted fish caught outside competition hours. A few years before that, there was the sneaky sod who nicked a huge bass from a public aquarium in a bid to win a big-money competition in the Channel Islands but was rumbled when, remarkably, a rival recognised the fish from a visit to the tourist attraction.

There can also be difficult times when you suspect something dodgy is happening – sometimes right under your nose – but you can't be certain and you know calling someone out is going to cause endless grief whether you are right or wrong.

I was once helping to officiate at a competition when an angler casually asked to check that I had taken a note of the two fish he claimed to have caught earlier. I hadn't seen him catch and didn't think I could have missed it.

But was I really going to challenge a guy I didn't know in front of others at a friendly comp? It wasn't beyond the bounds of possibility that I had been asleep at the wheel and not paying proper attention. I gave a non-committal shrug and didn't stop worrying until he was well out of contention.

It was an uncomfortable experience and I suppose that is why sometimes you cannot help wondering which is worst – the cheating itself, the suspicion or the wild rumours.

In recent times, I've heard of two sea anglers almost coming to blows after one accused the other of claiming extra length for every fish in a measure and release match, then having to apologise because he had mixed up inches and centimetres. It's also not too many years since a Scots angler was accused of using a maggot in a fly-fishing match.

I also recall being taken aside for *a quiet word* at a competition I was involved with and told that two boat partners had been overheard agreeing to add an extra five on their scorecards to how ever many trout they caught in that night's heat. The fact the person telling me this had missed out on qualifying by the rough length of FOUR fish might have been a clue.

And remember our guy, the one who supposedly came up with the cunning plan to plank a plastic bag of rainbows in a bush the night before a competition on a brown trout water? A year or so after that supposed incident, a story did the rounds that he had been caught shoving spark plugs – or pool balls in an alternative version of the rumour – down the gullets of trout to add a few vital ounces to their weight and had been threatened with joining the rest of the fish in the dam for his troubles.

Clearly then, cheating is not a laughing matter though I did find it hard not to smile when someone told me that a popular trick at coarse fishing matches in days past was to carry in small fish caught the day before in a FLASK.

Somewhere in the same postcode as cheating, but at a very different address, lives the whole question of fishing fibs. I could use the word lies because, let's be frank, that is what they are, but unless the untruths, exaggerations and fakery are causing genuine damage or hurt, the word seems a little harsh, or damning, somehow. Maybe that's because we all tell them or have told them at some point.

Sure, each of us likes to think it must be other, weaker-minded folk who are at it and that we are above that nonsense. But who among us can put hand on heart and say that we have NEVER let slip a fishing porkie? My favourite fishing writer, John Gierach, made that very point – and, unlike me, didn't hold back on choice of words – when he called one of his books All Fishermen Are Liars.

It might be no more than pointing someone in the wrong direction to protect a hotspot, or naming a different fly or bait to the one that is really catching. All of us will know someone who catches three trout, disappears to a quiet corner and comes back with their tally mysteriously up to 17. However mundane or even harmless it might be, a fib is still a fib.

Where it becomes difficult is when someone draws you into their lie and you are left with the awkward choice of telling one of your own to confirm theirs or exposing them as a phoney in front of others, neither of which is a desirable choice.

There was an affable Englishman I used to bump into occasionally on various trout waters and we'd always stop for a friendly chat. One day he invited me to a private water in the north of Scotland where he had won a day for two in a charity auction. I remember it as a particularly blowy morning and we had the place to ourselves, so we picked our way along one long shoreline with the wind at our backs, staying fairly close together. While he pulled lures and tried without success to tempt one of the water's big rainbows, I let Daddies bounce in the waves and managed to pick up a few nice brownies.

I only relate that because it is a fact and relevant to the story. I can say without hesitation that more often than not, I would have been the one to blank or catch fewer than the person I was out fishing with. Neither of us made a big deal of it and I finished a very pleasant day in fine company, impressed with the loch and the fish.

But that wasn't the end of it. Our paths didn't cross again for more than a year until a muggy June night when I got back to my car about half-ten to find three other guys – him included – packing up at their motors on a river closer to home. We got into conversation as tends to happen in the fading light of a classic fishy evening and, while comparing notes about various places, my old pal mentioned the loch we had been to and one of the others asked him what it was like.

"Great place. I took Mike there a while back," he said and I acknowledged that yes, it was a fine water.

But then he added: "Aye, the pair of us were lacing fish the whole day, mind?"

"Garbage," I said, laughing in his face. "You picked up the Blankety Blank cheque book and pen on the way out."

No, of course I didn't say that. It would have taken a special kind of callous coldness to dump on someone who had been generous enough to share fishing with me in the first place. Besides, it didn't sour my experience of the good day I'd had, so I gave a half nod, mumbled something about dries doing the trick and left him to enjoy whatever he was getting from his small flight of fancy.

Talking of untruths, I hope I have changed enough details in that story to make identification impossible.

That kind of false memory – deliberate or otherwise – is a close relative of another genre of fakery that I was reminded of when I was doing a round-up of unusual fishy presents for my Christmas column last year and came across a pair of fake tiny hands designed to make tiddlers look like monsters when they're posted online.

Now, we've all laughed at folk who use tricks like thrusting their arms out so the fish is closer to the camera and others who don't even make as much effort as that but simply post hero shots on social media while quoting weights that owe a large proportion to the imagination. Making fun of folk for doing all that – exaggerating fish size and/or numbers – is just part of the banter that makes the sport enjoyable and, luckily, most of us can take it as easily as we dish it out.

Sometimes, though, the mickey-taking and the sarcy jibes stop being funny and can turn vicious to the point where it starts to feel a little like bullying. Of course, you can argue that anyone who sets themselves up deserves all they get. But I've got to say I get a little uncomfortable when the slagging goes too far. I just feel that those quick to rain on the parade of others from the safety of their Samsung really need to think about the hurt they can cause, especially when they have no clue about the mental state of the person they are abusing.

I'm not a psychologist either so I cannot write a thesis on the deep-rooted motivations behind making out you have caught a few more fish than you really have, or adding a pound or two to your catch. I see it now and again in entries to the Prize Catch competition in my Scottish Sun column. Pike barely into double figures claimed as twenties, supposed 6lb trout lucky if they're half that.

For the folk who post exaggerated weights online or claim more than they have actually caught, maybe it is as simple as wanting to feel good about themselves, to walk back into the fishing hut a little bit taller. I guess there might be a little trace of inadequacy in the mix somewhere. In my experience, people in all of walks of life who have confidence in their ability – or just themselves – tend to have no problems dealing with their less successful moments. They embrace the setbacks and get on with it but we're not all made the same and perhaps some people need to talk up themselves and their fishing results for their own self-esteem.

Whatever the reasons for the exaggeration, does it really matter that much? Is it that big a deal? Why are some folk so keen to appoint themselves the angling police and expose to ridicule what they see as shortcomings in others? Is it really any of their business and how did they get to be so sure of their own perfection? Are they so confident they will never be caught in the what-goes-around-comes-around cycle?

The way I see it, a bit of banter is fine – and fun most of the time – but sometimes we maybe need to think about where to draw the line, especially when there is a much more serious fishing lie that doesn't attract anywhere near the same level of attention.

You see, all of the fibs I've mentioned so far – even the ones that are probably only apocryphal tales – have been about individuals who bend the truth for their own, sometimes dubious but often harmless, motivations. But the kind of lie I encountered last year is altogether more damaging. It can result in people being misled to the point that time, effort and money is wasted and reputations ruined.

It concerns Scotland's unluckiest salmon. Unlucky, or maybe just dumb, because it has been caught by anglers over and over again. Not just that either, because this particular salmon also defies the laws of nature and homing instinct by returning not just to the river of its birth like most others of its species, but somehow into different systems many miles and sometimes years apart.

This salmon is also in need of expert dietary advice because its weight has yo-yoed, sometimes by several pounds at a time. Crucially, each capture has been faithfully recorded on social media, mostly with a note of the date and time, the exact river and even pool, and the name of the fly it was tempted by. The fish I am thinking of weighed just over 12lb one time, had lost a pound when it next turned up but had put on nearly three a year later.

Oh, I must tell you the other very strange thing about this salmon. It only knows how to pose for the camera in one way and, even more odd, it is always pictured lying on familiar terrain next to very similar looking fishing rods. In fact, if you study the pictures carefully, you might say the backgrounds and the rods are actually identical, though sometimes mysteriously transformed into mirror images.

I am writing this in such an abstract way because other than the evidence of my own eyes, I cannot categorically prove that the same picture of the same salmon has turned up on social media on four separate occasions – well, four to my knowledge. Each time, it has been accompanied by a caption claiming that it was caught within the previous few days or couple of weeks at most.

I also cannot categorically prove that the purpose of this exercise is to convince anglers that a salmon trip to the X beat of the Y river might be worth a go because fish of this quality have been caught there recently, which means you have a chance of catching one too.

When I contacted one of the people who posted this salmon, on Facebook in his case, the explanation did not hold water, pardon the pun. The point of the picture, he insisted, was to show an example of the kind of salmon that were being caught on a particular river at a particular time. He also said salmon anglers were savvy enough to understand that it was not necessarily the actual fish described in the caption.

What? Seriously? Bear in mind that the person who made this statement was fairly prominent in the salmon fishing industry in Scotland. Had he really thought through what he had just told me? Are we really supposed to treat any online pic of a salmon as not necessarily genuine, even if it comes from a reputable source and has detailed information on where, when and how it was caught?

Sounded to me like he was saying salmon photos were like showhouses – just there to show what one might look like if we were lucky enough to catch it. When I pointed all this out, he went off on a different tack.

"You don't realise how hard it is to get hold of decent salmon pics."

No, stop, don't dig any deeper. If he's telling me it's difficult to get salmon pics because so few are around anymore, then that is the problem that needs to be tackled, as we are all only too well aware. I also understand the business case for talking up salmon beats but there is no excuse for trying to deceive anglers. It is lying and cheating, plain and simple. Just think how far Mark Antony and Cleopatra might have gone if camera phones had been around in their day.

Chapter 10

Turkish delight

L IKE many folk in these craziest of times, I've badly missed my holidays – which is another way of saying I've badly missed my holiday fishing. At least I can look back and bathe in the glow of a string of memorable moments in warmer climes, like narrowly escaping death at the hands of a poisonous monster and having a stand-off with a creature you wouldn't want anywhere near your hook. I've also encountered a Spanish hippy pimping out his girlfriend (or so I thought) and made a gruesome discovery that made me pack away my rod instantly and boycott local restaurants.

Just some of the joys of holiday fishing, the best way to fill that leisurely couple of hours in the late afternoon when

128

you've come back to the hotel room after a hard day's lazing by the pool, aimless wandering around the resort, or winding up the looky-looky men by trying on 14 shiny watches before telling them you're not interested. Your better half announces she is going to read for a bit on the balcony before getting ready for dinner, which both of you know translates as getting through a page and a half before her eyes droop and she sinks into a siesta.

It's tempting to follow suit, possibly accompanied by a beer and a Netflix episode instead of the book. On the other hand, the fishing gear you insisted on packing has been lying untouched at the back of the wardrobe since you got here a week ago and those rocks just down from the mini-golf look rather inviting.

Let me point out here that when I say holiday fishing, I'm not talking anything big league. This is not even in the same territory as doing hours of research and seeking out a grizzled, weather-beaten, chain-smoking skipper to take you out on an all-day deep-sea expedition where you'll end up strapped into a dentist's chair being beaten up by a 1,000lb bluefin tuna.

I'm not knocking that kind of adventure – that's dream-fishing stuff where you go properly equipped and steeled for the battle. I'll leave that kind of thing to my pal and fishing commando Alex Wilkie, aka The Rook, thanks very much.

To give you an idea of what I'm talking about, I'll run you through the gear I take on holiday. Telescopic rod that fits in the case diagonally, bog-standard spinning reel and a pouch containing a few floats, split-shot, small hooks and weights, scissors and disgorger. That's it. We are not in

Ernest Hemingway or even Rex Hunt country here.

Once in sunshine-land, I'll buy a baguette to pick apart for bait, find a harbour or easily accessible rocks and do some absolutely Primary One basic fishing. It's a plan and technique that has given me hours of relaxing, guess-the-species enjoyment in a string of destinations from the South of France to Lake Garda, Menorca to Cyprus, the Greek islands to Sorrento.

At least, it worked beautifully at a marina in Sorrento until two over-zealous *carabinieri* ordered me to cease and desist at gunpoint. Oh right, so that's what *Vietato Pescare* means.

There was no reason to suggest the same method would not work well from the rocks in Tenerife, which has become our most regular scorchio spot. But I changed tack first time I was there – and almost suffered badly for it. There was a fair old swell rolling into the horseshoe bay which is probably why I ditched the usual float and split shot rig and instead stuck on a little round ball weight to take the bait down.

Rather than one of the fine mullet that I had seen the locals pulling in, or any of the brightly coloured aquarium types I'd caught in other places, the first fish I landed was an ugly little critter – all thorns and spikes, like a scorpion with fins. I casually swung it towards me to grab carefully for unhooking – until I saw the looks of panic from a couple of Spaniards fishing a little bit along the rocks.

Now, communication was a slight problem. We were staying not in one of the bigger resorts where just about everyone speaks English, but on the outskirts of a fishing village still gamely resisting the encroaching apartment blocks and shiny hotels. Like a typical British tourist, it has never sunk in that if I'm going to be a guest in someone else's country on a regular basis, it might be polite to have a stab at learning more of the language beyond *gracias* and *larga beero por favor.*

Luckily, no words were necessary on this occasion. The frantic hand-waving, dramatic throat-clutching and scissors motions from Pedro and Carlos – excuse the casual stereotyping – got the message across to me that gripping the fish in my mitt might not be the smartest move. To their approving thumbs-ups and nods, I took the hint, snipped the line just above the hook and let the fish drop back into the water.

All became clear the next day when I stopped at a market stall selling fishing gear. The friendly Englishman behind the counter turned out to be a walking encyclopaedia of local fishing. He gave me some good advice on the best places to try as well as local techniques. As I was leaving, he asked: "By the way, do you know how to recognise the poison fish?"

Er, the what? He showed me a chart with many of the species native to the Canaries and I immediately recognised my potential nemesis. Turned out I had caught a Greater Weever, a nasty beast whose sting causes intense pain and, in rare cases, foaming at the mouth and even death. So gracias senors, I owe you several larga beeros.

Incidentally, as well as selling bits of tackle, the guy at the market stall was taking bookings for his boat trips which I managed to resist and, in fairness, he wasn't at all pushy. This bloke definitely knew his stuff and I'm sure he has plenty of satisfied customers but, a bit like the intentions of our pal the Greater Weever, I've been stung before by seaside boat trips.

As I mentioned earlier, I'm not talking about professional, properly equipped charter outfits but the ones you'll see in the harbours at any resort, aimed not at anglers in particular but at any passing tourist. They always have a couple of pics showing startled holidaymakers cradling giant beasts from the deep. If you look closely, they're usually wearing flared shorts and have 1980s haircuts.

The first time I fell for it was in Cyprus when, against my better judgement, I signed up for an evening outing at a quayside in Paphos. Yes, next to where the scrounging, ill-tempered pelicans strut their stuff. Even before we left harbour, I sensed the skipper couldn't care less now that he had our money. When a couple of raucous teenage lads in Engerland tops clambered on board, accompanied by Babycham-swigging, giggling girlfriends in tight summer dresses and high heels, I got the slightest inkling we weren't heading out for a serious fishing session.

It seemed we were barely clear of the moored yachts and pleasure boats when he dropped anchor and puffed nonchalantly on foul roll-ups while the handful of us who were actually interested in fishing pulled up the same small wrasse and sea bream we could just as easily have caught from the harbour wall.

It was several years before I gave into temptation again and then only because it seemed like every spot on the shore that I searched in our resort in Majorca was plastered with *Prohibo Pescar* signs.

I even enquired whether it was possible to buy a permit in the *Oficina de Informacion* at the harbour but my best efforts smashed into the language barrier.

"You wanna feesh? No problem, we sort it out," grinned the pleasant, efficient young chap behind the counter.

The form he got me to fill out seemed overly complicated for the sake of passing a few hours with my fishing rod and half a *hogaza*. Home address, passport number, species I intended to catch, did I know the rules on quotas…really? When I handed it back to him, he ran his eyes down it, ticked a lot of boxes, then nodded and asked: "OK, so what ees is the name, length and home port of your trawler?"

I'm not sure which of us was most annoyed at having our chain yanked and our time wasted.

Now that I think about it, there was one spot in that resort where there was no evidence of fishing being outlawed – a slow, narrow channel from the open sea which ran under the main promenade and emptied into a shallow basin infested with sea birds. The pond was also stuffed with a dense shoal of fat, lazy mullet which gathered under a bridge waiting for passers-by to drop in scraps of food.

OK, I admit it, I was tempted. Just a little bit. Come on, don't be too hard on me. I'd just trekked along a couple of miles of coastline in blistering heat searching in vain for a place where A, fishing was allowed and B, it wasn't mobbed with sunbathers. Now, here I was, wandering back to the hotel with my rod and tackle pouch still undisturbed and, sticking out of my back pocket, the crumpled-up form which the disgusted *informacion* guy had thrust at me. And there, right in front of me, a captive audience of big, obese fish.

No, you can't do it, whispered the little Oor Wullie angel on one shoulder. *It would be like hunting in a petting zoo.*

Go on, just a couple of casts, countered the horned devil on the other shoulder. *They're begging to be caught.*

Then fate intervened and made my mind up for me. A raggedy old geezer shuffled on to the bridge, a short, stout rod in one hand, a poly bag in the other. He elbowed his way past a couple of families with giggling little kids who were tossing popcorn down to the greedy, grateful mullet. Without ceremony, he dropped down his line with baited hook and, within a matter of seconds, swung a fish of maybe a couple of pounds up and over the bridge railing. He smacked it violently against the balustrade, tore out the hook roughly and dropped it into the bag. As the parents and children watched horrified, he repeated the process twice and caved in the heads of two more naïve mullet in quick succession. This was carnage – and that's the kids I'm talking about. One screamed, two started crying.

"The bad man's murdering our fish," wailed another.

The *bad man* couldn't care less. He reeled in, tucked his hook in the cork handle and went back the way he had come, dinner sorted. I shook my head like an offended saint and muttered words like *dreadful* and *giving anglers a bad name* as I crossed the bridge among the parents consoling their distraught little ones.

It seemed that if I wanted to fish on that Majorcan holiday, there was nothing for it but to book a slot on one of the boats advertised on the booths at the front. I tried hard to ignore the pic of the grinning kid with the huge fish on the side and tried even harder to ignore the virtual guarantee of the gap-toothed, patter-merchant of a skipper.

It goes without saying that I should have known better.

FISHING IN THE SUN

As it turned out, there were only two paying customers that morning, myself and a likeable bloke from the English Midlands looking for something a tad livelier than his regular Sunday canal session on the bream. We managed one skittery, foul-hooked baby barracuda between us after parting with 70 euros each for what amounted to a leisurely, four-hour, sightseeing boat ride along the coast and back. We were only able to lighten the mood by running a friendly sweep on how many times the skipper would reprise his Oscar-nominated, stunned and amazed, *ah dun unerstan* performance and tell us we should have seen it yesterday. Right, definitely no more tourist-magnet boat trips for me then.

Not that shore fishing hasn't had its drawbacks. Like the day back in my little bay in Tenerife, a year or so after the poison fish encounter, when I ended up with something even more unwelcome on my line.

I was fishing from what had become a regular haunt of mine – a shelf of rock under a row of fish restaurants next to a square jutting out from the promenade – waiting to see what would take the cube of bread first. One of the great joys of holiday fishing in foreign parts is that you often have no idea what is lurking down there and might grab hold. Which is fine, as long as you are talking about fish – not a hulking great TURTLE.

It was bigger than a bin lid and surfaced without warning a foot from my float. The moment I saw it, I tried to flick the bright, red-tipped waggler out of harm's way but the sudden movement must have made the creature panic because it splashed about wildly, got the line caught round its leg and shot off like a bullet in the direction of the open sea. I had no control over it whatsoever and for the first time I can remember since I took up fishing, I was rocked by a feeling of utter helplessness. I honestly did not have the first clue what to do.

I swear I could almost hear my lightweight holiday rod howling in pain as it bent into a test curve it definitely was not designed to withstand. As I waited for it to snap, first 50, then 100, then all 150 yards of line tore off my reel. I can only guess it was the jolt as the line came to an end on the empty spool that made the turtle come to a matching, abrupt halt way out in the middle of the bay and start thrashing around in the breakers. If it had kept on going, the rod would have broken, no question.

Now it became a classic stand-off. The turtle stopped shaking and just floated defiantly on the surface, refusing to budge. It was either figuring out its next move or waiting to see what I was going to do, though I'm probably crediting the species with more thought process than it actually has. Even so, it was most definitely all about who blinked first and I had no choice but to simply hold on to the rod.

What wasn't helping was the small but enthralled audience that had assembled above my rocky perch. Two mums, assorted kids and a handful of pensioners leaned over a rail, pointing first at me, then the turtle, then back at me, giving it their best firework display *oohs* and *aahs*.

I weighed up the options and neither offered a positive outcome. Did I try to fight it to a standstill? In the unlikely event that I was able to win back all of that 6lb breaking strain line and somehow haul it up on to the rocks, what the hell was I supposed to do with 30-40lb of angry, snapping turtle? Should I cut the line then? Of course not, that was out of the question. There was no way I could leave the innocent creature with nearly 150 yards of nylon trailing from it. Aside from the moral considerations, who needs the hassle of animal welfare zealots putting up wanted posters all over the Canaries?

Then, as I clung on desperately – still clueless – the drama was suddenly all over without me having to make a decisive move. The turtle had somehow freed itself and was gone as if it had never been there. My audience, let down by the anti-climax, also dispersed quickly before I even had the chance to take a bow.

My other clueless moment in Tenerife came a few miles along the Adeje coast, on the day a young guy tried to swap his girlfriend for a fish. Blame the language barrier again, blame too much heat, but honestly, it really did look to me like I was being asked to trade a mullet for a curly-haired Spanish beauty.

There I was, minding my own business, passing a couple of happy hours fishing way out on a long finger of piled up rocks that forms a breakwater next to a beach, while my wife enjoyed a peaceful pre-dinner snooze back at the hotel.

My go-to bait for the grey mullet found all around these shores is bread or dough but I've discovered that when they turn shy, especially in the more heavily-fished locations, little chunks of bacon on small hooks can sometimes save the day. It's catch and release on holiday, of course, because apart from having no desire to kill them, I can't imagine wandering into the hotel foyer in 25C heat with a bag of ripe fish would be an overly popular move.

So, as I say, I'm having a fun afternoon, lazily hooking maybe one in eight or nine of the mullet that jab lightning fast at the lardons, then getting a nice bend in the rod as flashes of silver glint in the lime-green water. I was in the act of dropping the third fish back into the depths when a head popped up to my right and, too late, a guy began waving a hand and yelling "No". He was probably mid-thirties, friendly face, hair in braids and wearing the kind of bohemian clobber I associated with the band of folk who sat at the side of pavements in the resort with acoustic guitars and bottles of wine, wreathed in a musky aroma familiar from my student days.

In good but heavily-accented English, he explained he had been fishing for his supper a little bit further along the rocks – out of sight to me – but with no success. He pointed dolefully after the disappearing fish, rubbed his stomach theatrically and said: "La cena…er, dinner."

Then he held out a pack of cigarettes and added: "Next one…I buy, er, swap?"

When I smiled and told him I didn't smoke, he looked thoughtful for a moment then pointed back the way he'd come and called out something incomprehensible.

Next thing, a sultry beauty, maybe a little younger than him, popped her head above the rock where they had planted themselves. The guy babbled something rapidly at her then went into a little pantomime of pointing at me, making the shape of a fish with his hands, then gesturing towards her. That was when the negotiation, to me at least, moved into decidedly dodgy territory. He pointed back at the girl, then at me again, then gave a thumbs up. Honestly, if you thought I was nervous about the poison fish and the turtle…

The girl's response was what really put me in panic

mode. She waved, a coy smile spreading into a wide grin, then held out a hand in the shape of a claw, shook her wrist gently and nodded as if sealing the arrangement. I couldn't help thinking, rubbish deal for her – pale Scots guy just turned 60 with a dodgy heart and a RyanAir return ticket.

Then all became clear when she wandered over, holding out some little arty-crafty bracelets she'd been making with string and shells. She tapped my wrist and said: "For your meessus maybe?"

It was time for me to head back anyway so I handed over the rest of the lardons and some small hooks then left them to it. But I still wonder how my wife would have reacted if I'd wandered back to our hotel room and said: "Er, dearest, meet Luciana. I got her for two fish."

That guy would not have been so quick to trade his cigarettes and certainly not his girlfriend's wares – I'm talking about the DIY bracelets now – for the fish I targeted during another holiday in Turkey. Honestly, you will not like the reason why. In fact, if you're reading this over breakfast, skip over the page to the next chapter.

For a change, I'd brought a fly-fishing set-up with me, starting with a seven-piece Shakespeare I thought of as my poacher's rod, though I've never used it for that purpose – honest. I'd been giving a lot of thought to trying the fly in saltwater and figured if it didn't work, I could always stick a spinning reel on the rod and go back to basics. Not ideal, but doable.

It seemed the fates were with me. The place where we were staying had a channel running parallel to the sea, separating the restaurants and bars that lined the prom and a bustling network of shops and stalls. There was a hub of jetties in the channel where you could step on and off water taxis or book boats for all-day island tours. But two or three minutes from the centre of the resort, it got fairly quiet. Better still, fish were showing all over the place, rising to take on the surface or head-and-tailing to feed just below it. Yes, my old pals the mullet again and these were seriously chunky fish which, the evidence of my eyes suggested, might well take a fly.

What followed was sheer frustration for three days as these fish refused to look at anything that I put in front of them. I hadn't brought a huge number of flies but there was a decent variety. I tried nymphs and wets in an attempt to vaguely represent the grubs and insects I could actually see. I tried bushy dries and tiny dries because they were definitely taking something off the top. I tried flashy lures to spark a reaction, old faithful Damsels and Cats and Dancers. Nought. Not a spark of interest.

Right, location then. Perhaps it was still too busy where I was fishing. I only saw the very occasional other angler but there were a handful of fishermen out on small boats with nets, presumably selling their catches to the numerous restaurants dotted all along the prom.

So, I started walking and kept on going, in the opposite direction of the channel's flow. The further I ventured, the more fish I saw, greedily feeding on...what? Then I found the answer and seriously wished I hadn't.

I must have walked the best part of a mile when I glimpsed a pool up ahead, right on a bend, that was thick with fish. An old cliché popped into my head, the one about how there were so many fish, you could have walked across their backs. Just round the bend, there it was – the source of their feast and one hatch I could never match. A sewage pipe, spilling raw human waste into the channel and the fish couldn't get enough of it.

I thought about the guys out with their nets and, funnily enough, I avoided mullet on the restaurant menus for the rest of that holiday.

Chapter 11

Tope of the world

THERE is something about being in a confined space on a boat deck with an angry shark that I will never get used to. It's one part euphoric, one part chaotic, one part scary. But overall, simply awe-inspiring. It's that small window when you, or another angler on board, has won the muscle-straining battle with a tope four or five feet long and suddenly it's hauled on board and at your feet. The adrenaline rush is infectious and your heart, or the heart of whoever has been attached to this beast for the last 10 or 15 minutes, is racing faster than everyone else's.

The skipper is hugely experienced and for him this is all part of the job, so logically there isn't any serious danger. Take the logic a step further and you remember it's a tope, so far down the shark pecking order it probably wouldn't even get an extra's role in a Jaws remake. But still, it's a shark and it's out of its natural habitat which means it's hacked off at you and everyone else forming the tight circle around it.

And here's the thing, any second now you're going to have to take hold of it and you mustn't hesitate. You can't say *No* because you don't want to go through all that effort and not have the evidence of a pic and anyway, if you're not prepared to deal with the tope, then maybe you have no business trying to catch it in the first place. Plus, you'd never live it down. *What, scared of a baby shark?* There is no time to prepare yourself either because this whole operation is against the clock. Like all good anglers, you, the skipper and everyone else on board all care about your quarry's wellbeing and the longer it is out of the water, the less its chances of surviving the ordeal you are putting it through.

Right, no messing about, a firm *Yes* when the skipper asks if you're ready and suddenly you're cradling this shark firmly and grinning – or is it grimacing? – for the hero shot as mobiles click all around. Then the tope is eased over the side, gently slid back into the water and all that intense concentration and sheer physical strain melt away. The whole episode, from hauling the fish aboard to careful release, lasts less than a minute but it reminds me yet again why I have had a lifelong love affair with fishing from boats on Scottish shores.

If I ever stop to consider my top angling experiences, I surprise myself because I feel they should exclusively involve trout and flies, my default type of fishing and what

I do 80 per cent of the time I'm on or around water. But what actually jumps into my head first and is always a serious contender in the best-moments category, is one particular scene, or rather an amalgam of similar scenes repeated at various points in my life, from Loch Long as a small boy to the last time I was waiting for the first pollock beneath the Mull of Galloway lighthouse.

It needs a bit of back story, this scene, but it's probably sufficient to go back no further than the night before a fishing trip when you've made the call to the skipper to check the weather is OK and which harbour or beach you are setting out from. A quick round of texts with the other guys making the trip, including the one you are meeting halfway at the supermarket car park. A fitful, kids-on-Christmas-Eve sleep followed by a stealthy departure in the early morning dark when, because you're a decent human being, you try not to bang the boot lid and doors in case you wake up the civilians, i.e., your neighbours.

Then the drive across country while the new day slowly reclaims the light and the world is reborn once more. The spirits-lifting first glimpse of sea when you hit the coast road. The meet-up at the harbour, old and recent acquaintances alike renewed. The carting of gear from cars to boat like a DIY flitting.

There's a lot of bluster, bravado and mutual taunting in the next, phoney war part of the day while you're getting your sea legs amidst the diesel fumes and the harbour wall shrinks in the distance over your shoulder. After what feels like an age, the engine coughs to a halt and the skipper says something like: "Right boys, down you go."

OK, this moment right here is what I'm talking about.

FISHING IN THE SUN

The banter stops abruptly, the laughter dies, the throbbing of the twin motors has gone and after the plopping of weights entering water, there is nothing. A kind of spell descends, a hush that is so eerie you feel you could touch it. The silence is so loaded and thick you could hear a safety-snap swivel drop. As the boat finds its own see-saw rhythm in the grey, rolling waves, no one is interested in conversation.

There is absolute concentration as eyes shift to rods, upright in their holders, and everyone tries to locate that groove where you can tell the difference between the natural swing of the tips in the swell and a fish at your bait. It is as if no one is daring to speak for fear of tempting fate. You tell yourself it's not a competition but all the same you'd like to get a fish early doors and get the spectre of a blank off your back.

Then, with unmistakable excitement in their voice, someone on the other side of the boat shouts: "That's me."

They wrench the rod from the holder, start pumping and the spell is broken. It's business as usual as everyone else waits with eager anticipation to see that first fish and silently urges their rod to be the next one called into action.

That usually brief scene of stillness and quiet is like a Groundhog Day for me which I can trace all the way back to a family holiday in Arbroath when I was eight or nine. The reason it is important is probably something to do with not getting on well with my old man for long parts of my adult life, so memories of great fishing days with him become positive nuggets to cling on to now that he is no longer around for the fracture to be healed. This isn't Oprah, so we'll leave the daddy issues there, thanks very much.

Strangely enough, for the numerous good trips that were to follow, my maiden voyage is still marked down in our family annals as a disaster at sea and occasionally recounted like some Moby Dick epic. My father had booked a 6pm fishing trip, just the two of us. But we found ourselves behind schedule after a busy day doing all the usual seaside stuff with the rest of the family. We rushed back to the boarding house where we wolfed down a dinner of greasy liver and onions – a relevant detail never missed from the story – then had a mad bolt through the streets of the seaside town to the harbour to catch the boat with seconds to spare.

What followed was four miserable hours of my old man and me hanging over the side with our churning, bloated bellies on full spin cycle, retching until there was nothing left to give up to the waves. Somewhere amidst the agony, there was a small, solitary saithe spinning in the air, possibly on the end of my line but tangled up with someone else's, not that I cared by that point.

My most vivid recollection is of curling up on the floor of the boat, gripping my knees tightly, and the skipper coming over and leaning in to speak to me. In my head, he was ancient with his thick, white beard, but my dad later told me he was no more than 40. What I remember most is the skipper tapping his temple as he told me that being sea sick was all in the head. For some reason it sticks in my mind that he pronounced it seek.

"Just decide right now," he said gently. "Tell yourself that you're never going to feel *seek* on a boat ever again in your life."

Funnily enough, more than half a century and countless sea fishing trips later, he was right – touch wood.

146

We had other more successful seafaring adventures after that, my old man and me. He got into sea angling in a big way for a while and joined a fishing club at the Daily Record, where he worked, which led me into regular, more serious outings as well as an early brush with newspapers. The romantic in me could call it a ritualistic passing-on of ink in the veins, I suppose.

The sea trips left from the printworks in Glasgow at dawn on Sunday mornings so he would take me into work with him on the Saturday night. While he did his shift as a printer, I would go out on one of the delivery vans with a driver who was also in the fishing club.

I remember Big Peter steering us right into the heart of Central Station, giving folk crowding the concourse no option but to part to let him through. Then he would lug tied-up bundles of early editions as if they were weightless and chuck them on to trains bound for far-flung outposts like Stranraer and Dumfries.

For an impressionable youngster, it was thrilling enough to be at the centre of the noisy hustle and bustle of a Saturday night in 1960s Glasgow but then Big Peter laid on a bonus. He casually tossed a dozen or so hot-off-the-press Sunday Mails on to the seat beside me and said: "There's your pocket money, wee fella."

First time out I was baffled until a procession of late-night revellers, in various states of sobriety, spotted the van with the title in huge letters on the side and knocked on the window.

"Any chance of a paper, pal?"

They would thrust bundles of loose change at me from their drunk man's pockets so they could browse the back

147

pages on the way home to Pollok or Paisley or Port Glasgow.

Those outings with the Daily Record club were where I first discovered that little oasis of silence, sometimes made spookier by an early morning sea mist. Perhaps the quiet stillness at the start of the fishing made such an impression because our boat companions were hard, gallus, working men who spent the rest of the day firing scathing wit and loud, crude curses back and forward, while the dads among them warned us kids to cover our ears every two minutes. Naturally, we youngsters took a vicarious delight in the language – the more foul and lurid, the better.

The main attraction was, of course, catching more and bigger fish than I could have imagined, mainly cod with the occasional haddock, pollock and coalie. This was in the days before the Clyde was trawled to a standstill and reduced by greed to a virtual marine desert.

But other incidents stand out too, like the morning our boat broke down in a big chop and we had to literally walk the plank as we transferred to a substitute vessel via a flimsy, rocking and rolling gangway.

Another time, we were booked on a Loch Long charter a few days after the skipper had broken the Scottish conger record. When we boarded, there were half a dozen eels laid over the side of the boat which looked huge to me. But he swept them into the water and muttered contemptuously: "Boot laces."

Later that same day, after hours of non-stop, arm-aching action hauling fish up from the bottom, the same skipper, Red Eric, beckoned me to the back of the boat. He traced an arc with his finger and told me I was witnessing a rare phenomenon – hundreds if not thousands of mackerel leaping and splashing on the surface in the afternoon sunshine after being chased up through the layers by predators.

He handed me a dinky fibre-glass Daiwa spinning rod with a small silver Mepp and told me to cast it among the frantic mackerel. Looking back, this guy was a visionary – the fight on light gear was sensational.

Like a lot of folk, my boat trips – and much of my fishing generally – were curtailed considerably while my own kids were small, with a few notable exceptions.

There was an extraordinary trip out of Ayr with my then teenage stepson, Paul. We came home with so many mackerel that within a couple of days, neighbours were closing their curtains or sitting in darkened houses, pretending they weren't home when we went round the doors trying to give them away.

Then there was the ultimate sod's law outing with a bunch of colleagues not long after I started on The Scottish Sun back in the early 1990s. It was an unofficial, team-bonding bit of fun really and the guys who turned up in everyday anoraks and work shoes – and didn't know one end of a rod from the other – treated it as a carry-on and caught fish effortlessly all day, including herring on bare hooks.

The two self-proclaimed "proper anglers", myself and a sadly-departed tabloid genius by the name of Tim Harper, turned up kitted out in our brand name fishing jackets, camo waterproof over-trousers and a riot of gear including multi-coloured rubber lures – or *pink worms* as they became in the post mortem slagging match. Inevitably, neither of us could summon up a bite all morning and we were ripped to shreds by a bunch of newspaper jackals not generally renowned for their sensitivity.

The spark that got me back into boat fishing a decade or so ago was the annual struggle to think of an original Christmas present for the aforementioned Paul.

By that stage, he had grown into a living advert for his profession as a tattoo artist of considerable repute – and my No 1 choice for company on a day's fishing. We don't go out together nearly often enough, mainly because he has stuck with the coarse and predator roots picked up from the times we lived down south, while I have drifted into what he considers the more precious realms of fly fishing. (Believe me, he puts it much less politely than that.)

So, two birds with one stone, I got him a voucher for a day's shark fishing for Christmas. Figuring it would be rude not to tag along, I bought another one and saved my wife the bother of what to get me for my birthday four days later which, coincidentally, I share with Paul.

So began a series of regular jaunts as far south as you can go in Scotland without falling off the edge, to spend fabulous days on the Mull of Galloway with Onyer Marks charters.

That first trip turned into one of those days when everything fell into place, right from the drive down the coastline from Girvan through murk and rain that made us wonder if we'd brought enough waterproofs, before it suddenly turned dry and pleasantly mild as we pulled into tiny Port Logan.

We were a couple of hours out at sea when I realised why Onyer Marks have earned such a soaring reputation. Much

150

of this was new to us so we'd had our fun hauling up mackerel and herring to fill the bait tub and were now trying to get our heads round the tope rigs, swivels, beads and booms, while the boat bounced its way to the shark grounds.

This was the serious business, what we had come for, and before long one of the four rods twitched and line started paying out, clicking on the ratchet. Skipper Ian Burrett's face creased, a study in concentration, before he confidently informed us what kind of fish was making a meal of the half-mackerel down in the depths and its likely size. I got the feeling that if pushed, he would tell you what it had for breakfast, its star sign and its top five favourite movies.

That's what a knowledge of these waters spanning 30 years does and aside from his invaluable expertise, he's also a very good skipper because he quickly susses out the fishermen he has on board. How much help they need, how much they want to be left to their own devices, and all done with good humour, infinite patience and infectious enthusiasm.

It was Paul's mate, Max, who got the first tope on that trip after a tense, all-action battle which ended with him cradling a 34lb belter which gave him a smile that didn't shift all day. Best and proudest moment for me was seeing my daughter Laura, who completed our crew that first time, take on an even bigger tope. Legs planted, she clung on grimly and did outstandingly well to fight it into submission.

Only downside was a bout of camera shyness – from the tope, not Laura – that left her without a picture as the fish took a leap for freedom just as it was being lifted into the boat. Skipper Ian gave it a shade under 40lb though Max, his own tope safely recorded, risked being chucked overboard by murmuring: "Yeah, but we'll never really know, will we?"

Despite our best efforts, the tope decided to stop playing after that but Paul and I were more than happy to settle for some big bull huss which fought as much on the boat as in the water. We knew we'd back for another crack at the tope.

And we have returned, many times over the years, with varying degrees of success and always with stories to take back as well as memories of good fish caught. Paul and I have been the constants but the other faces have changed.

My pal Craig joined us once and as well as catching a fair few fish, spent the day grinning and laughing at the excitement of it all. Another mate, Jim, came along and tamed the tope like a pro, cool as you like.

Max brought his son Leon one time and he had a starring role in what became known, to us anyway, as the Year of the Seal.

These furry hooligans invariably pop up to give us grief and destroy our gear at some point in each trip. They hang 30 or 40 yards off the boat, staring us out, letting us do half the job for them, because I am convinced that they have learned to watch for a rod bending before taking off after our battling, writhing fish. If they catch up before we get our fish on board, they'll snaffle the rigs along with their lunch, seemingly impervious to the hooks they collect for their trouble. Paul does not hold back in either the colour or the volume of his wrath when he falls victim. We're lucky other boats in the vicinity don't think they're picking up a distress call.

But back to Leon, then 17 and a first-time angler who was struggling to get the timing bang on with the pollock that were making his float jab under. Finally, he hooked one – his first ever fish – but Paul spotted that our heavyweight stalker had already taken off in pursuit. We urged Leon to reel in as fast as he could. (I'll leave the actual words to your imagination...not difficult.) He did well, staying just ahead of the huge, dark shape in hot pursuit. Leon swung the fish out of the water and Max was already reaching over to slap his son's shoulders in a proper proud dad moment while Paul and I roared out congratulations.

But the good vibe was premature. The seal came hurtling out of the froth and hung in the air like a soccer striker as it swallowed the lot – fish, rig and even float – before flipping back into the water. It had been so close we could have reached out and touched it. I felt bad for Leon but there would be more fish. This had been nature in the raw, a genuine holy sh*t moment, and worth the entrance money alone.

Also good entertainment value was my mate Kenny, who came along the following year. Yes, the same Kenny who was convinced I was putting myself at risk from serial killers by staying out fishing on my own after dark. As I explained, he is an out-and-out townie who thinks a public park is a close relative of an Amazon rain forest, but a top guy with boundless enthusiasm who had jumped at the chance when a slot on the boat opened up late on.

As all anglers know, we're kids at heart and it's almost impossible to sleep before a big trip but Kenny took it to extremes. It had just gone 7am and I wasn't even at Girvan – halfway on my journey – when I got the first call.

"Mike, where's this cattle grid you told me to watch out for?"

Anyone who has ever launched from the beach on the windy road to the Mull of Galloway lighthouse will know what he was on about. He was a full two hours early for our 9am kick-off.

Once at sea, he barely survived his first ordeal – the fake custom I'd cooked up with Ian's son, Matty, our skipper for the day. We told Kenny that boats were cursed unless debut anglers bit the head off the first fish they caught and swallowed it.

He stared long and hard at the first mackerel, gripped in his leather gloves – yes, gloves – before apologising profusely because he couldn't go through with it and promising he'd try again later.

With that unfailing fishing cliché – beginner's luck – he got the first tope run and found himself attached to a seriously big beast. Cheeks puffed, sheer terror on his face, he begged one of us to take over. But we refused, told him it was his fish and ordered him to get on with it. To his credit, he buckled down and was gradually winning the war of attrition when he learned the hard, sickening lesson we all experience from time to time.

Without warning, the line went slack and the fish was gone. Still shaking, he reeled in to find his hook almost straightened. Matty reckoned the tope responsible had been at least twice the size of the 33-pounder I caught a few minutes later.

Still frazzled and beaten up from the trauma, Kenny's response was to stagger backwards into the cabin, flop on to the seat and sleep like a baby for two solid hours. Losing a fish like that is sore but at least he was spared having to bite its head off.

Chapter 12

Heaven and Perth

RIGHT, your children are in their late teens, starting their first job or maybe halfway through university, so they're thinking about fleeing the nest. If you want my advice – and don't tell my wife I said this – encourage them to spread their wings and not feel they have to settle down too close to home. Not that I don't love my weans and I'll always be a regular visitor wherever they lay their hats. But the spin-off from spending quality time with my grown-up kids in different parts of the country is that it brings so many more trout waters within reach.

As fishing bases go, it's hard to beat the Perth area where my youngest daughter Laura lives. The choice of fly fishing within an easy half-hour's drive is mouth-watering, up the range to an hour and there's enough to keep you going almost indefinitely.

If you are looking for another bonus still, Perthshire is simply a wonderful place to go fishing. To my mind, it is the prettiest of Scotland's olden-day counties. The Big Country, as some people call it, produces ever-shifting but always stunning works of nature's art with the changing of the seasons. In an earlier chapter, I mention the million-dollar beach view from my mate's croft in Lewis. The sweeping, spectacular vista from the top floor window of my daughter's house in Crieff could give it a run for its money any day.

Here are my impressions of just a few of the trout waters in the area that I have visited over the last few years. For the final pair of fisheries, I have to admit to playing fast and loose with the chapter heading as I nipped over the county border – just – into Kinross.

GLENFARG, OCTOBER 2015.

Sometimes the best days come when you're not expecting much, especially when it's a water you don't have a clue about, the weather is lousy and you were in two minds about going out fishing in the first place. I'd had Glenfarg reservoir in the back of my mind since someone mentioned it to me a few years earlier and the stars seemed to align when the name popped up again in an email exchange just as I happened to be staying close by and had a free afternoon.

I wasn't long back at work after a big heart op so I was gradually getting used to the pace of newspapers again. On my days off, I wasn't exactly bursting with energy and it would have been easy to succumb to a bout of general lethargy. The miserable, non-stop rain wasn't exactly inviting but I had the urge to get back fishing regularly again and the alternative was wasting the day.

So, Glenfarg it was then, though the exhaust-threatening track from the country road to the car park didn't do much to lift my spirits. Neither did the clearly neglected, weed-choked pond I came across, which might have made me turn back there and then if I hadn't quickly discovered, to my relief, that it wasn't the fly water.

Then, out of all this downbeat misery, a kind of uplifting joy. I turned a corner after the five-minute stroll from the car park and found myself looking at a little corner of rural heaven – a delightful stretch of water that you could easily mistake for a wild Highland lochan. All little nooks and crannies and even its own island, adding up to the sort of place where we anglers feel privileged to conduct our sport – with the added bonus of having it to myself.

Right on cue the rain stopped, the wind dropped a few notches and a couple of trout poked their heads out of the water to see who had come to interrupt their relaxation. Suddenly, all was right with the world again.

For the first couple of hours, the trout rose steadily enough to flies on the surface in a gentle ripple, with a static olive CDC and a black Bob's Bits sharing the honours. When the breeze got up again, a Sedge tweaked through the wave got the most regular response. But the real plus was that when the rise petered out, it was still about naturals.

It was a bit of a jolt to stop and realise how seldom wet flies form the first line of attack these days. If dries aren't doing the business, I'll usually turn to nymphs, Buzzers or mini-lures, so it was a joy to blow away the cobwebs on the wets box and use the traditionals I learned to fly fish with. Even better, the trout didn't need tricked up variants. They were more than happy to wolf down bog-standard Kates, Bibios and Pennels.

My only question mark over Glenfarg that first time was why they bothered to stock rainbows when there was such a healthy head of resident brown trout. Over two sessions – I liked the place so much I came back a few days later – I caught at a ratio of five brownies for each bow and they were all solid, plucky fighters.

August 2017.

I became rather attached to Glenfarg but we nearly fell out on one later visit when I came very close to discarding my self-imposed dry flies first rule.

I freely admit an addiction to top-of-the-water sport and I know I'm not alone in that so it takes a lot for me to start a different way. One year I even turned a self-imposed target of catching on dries in every month into a quest that bordered on the obsessive.

It had seemed a no-brainer when I drove down the now familiar track to Glenfarg on a warmish late summer's evening with ample cloud cover, plenty of insect life in evidence and enough of a breeze to ensure there would be a decent ripple...just about every box ticked. Well, every box except the one next to rising fish.

Not one movement did I see as I scanned the water on the walk to my usual starting spot on the point just down from the lodge. I tell a lie. There was one head-turning splash that gave me hope...till the duck resurfaced a few seconds later.

No evidence of fish feeding on the surface so no logical

reason to start with flies on the surface, right? Then a little bell went off, a reminder that fishing dries blind can work. I thought back to a night at Carron Valley during a qualifier for the Masters competition I used to be involved with. The heat was won by a very experienced angler who told me his successful tactic had been just that – persisting with dries even though next to nothing had been showing. That didn't stop the fish coming up for his flies readily.

Funnily enough, I also remembered him telling me it only got difficult late in the evening when the trout did start rising en masse.

OK, worth a go then and to my mind, using dries when no trout are showing takes two things – blind faith, literally, and a big, bushy fly. The point is, there is no way to match exactly what the fish are feeding on and you can only take an educated guess as to where they might be. The trick then, is to lure your quarry to the top with something that looks not only enticing but worth the effort and energy expended – and it only needs one fish to look up.

With that in mind, I teamed up a Size 10 Grunter on the point with a Yellow Owl one size down on the dropper. Thankfully, it didn't take long to find some encouragement as a trout battered the Grunter within seconds of it hitting the water. That one didn't stick but the next one a few minutes later did – a typical Glenfarg rainbow of just under 2lb which only woke up when it was almost in the net then scrapped like it had been slapped into a response.

What I was really after though, were the wild brownies I'd encountered on previous visits to Glenfarg. They are lovely fish – gold-tinted, hard little fighters that provide superb sport on a light rod.

The action was frantic for the first 40 minutes or so then a dip in temperature made it more difficult and sporadic but no less fascinating for that. Rather than casting for the sake of casting, it became about stealthy patrolling in search of the merest sign of life. First cast to any flicker of activity was invariably the best chance of an offer if not a hook-up.

POSTSCRIPT: With fishing as much fun as this, it surprised me that over the four times I visited Glenfarg, I only ever saw two other anglers. Sure, it's hard to beat having such a compact, out-of-the-way water all to yourself as a kind of personal playground. But I couldn't help feeling other fly fishers didn't know what they were missing – particularly that night when all they needed was blind faith.

Last I heard, Glenfarg was being operated as a private syndicate and that didn't come as a surprise given the lack of paying customers I observed. Good luck to whoever is involved. I can't think of many better waters to have as an exclusive trout sanctuary.

ORCHILL, JULY 2016.
There is a masochistic streak in anglers, I'm convinced of it. There's the horrific weather we will go out in, the sleep we will give up to be on the water early, the mental pain we put up with when the fish aren't being co-operative. And another one: we think difficult is OK. In fact, we embrace difficult because when fishing stops being a challenge, it's probably time to think about chucking it, buying yourself a smart blazer and taking up old man's bowls. (I know, I know, I keep being told bowls is a sport for all ages. I'm just picking on it because a couple of players shouted at my dog to keep off their precious green

when it was 30 yards away and not even thinking about it.)

Where were we? Oh yes, my old acquaintances, masochism and difficulty, because I didn't go to Orchill and catch fish non-stop. The trout were not exactly shoving each other aside to climb all over my flies. In truth, I found the fishery, just outside Braco, Perthshire, a tough nut to crack. Very tough, in fact. And I loved every minute of it.

I daresay there are times when you can pop into Orchill, hit it just right and catch in numbers and with ease. But a muggy summer's evening with the temperature high and barely a breath of wind was never going to be easy, especially when there's so much natural feeding in this lush little loch that the trout need barely give even the most convincing artificial a second look.

As a result, it becomes an endurance test but an enjoyable one because the fact you are not seeing many other rods bend is both troubling and reassuring at the same time. Troubling because it means the fish are being ultra-fussy and playing hard to get. Reassuring because you're not alone in finding it tough which means that maybe you're not such a numpty after all.

On that kind of day, you try everything in your repertoire to tempt a trout. Just one will do for starters and when it happened, and the fish took the white Owl I'd ambushed it with by sussing out its route of travel, I allowed myself a moment of quiet self-congratulation, a silent *well played son.*

It's a kind of satisfaction level, to me at least, that is right up there with the days when everything goes right and the fish keep coming. I managed a few more, each time landing a big, bright fly right on the nose of a fish in the hope it would snap at it through sheer annoyance if not hunger.

All in all, a worthwhile if not prolific session. So why do I rate Orchill so highly? Well, it's certainly one of the prettiest fisheries I've been to – a reminder that our sport takes us to special places which is a factor that should always be appreciated.

Owners Elizabeth and Andrew Jackson are proper fishing folk who know anglers and make them feel at home. They also make sure the surroundings remain neat and attractive, the water in good nick so that the fish they stock fight like demons once the loch's free, natural larder toughens them up.

But more than that, there is something else about Orchill that is harder to define. It just feels like a good place to be. A place where it feels right to be fishing. If you're not sure what I mean by that, there is only way to find out.

POSTSCRIPT: Over the years I have compiled a steadily growing mental list of trout waters I call my Arnies. Places where I pack my gear into the car when the fishing is done, put on my best Terminator voice and, after checking no one is listening, make myself a promise: *I'll be back.*

I'm thinking of places like Carron Valley with its magical summer evenings, Harelaw, where you could spend an entire season and still not unlock all of its secrets, Parkview, which took me surprise, Glenfarg – see above – and a few others besides. I added another one that evening and, in fact, Orchill shot right up the must-return list.

WILLOWGATE, JULY 2016.
Surely it isn't just me who gets songs in their head while

163

fishing and, actually, it's not even full songs most of the time, just a couple of lines from the verse or the chorus. Why they lodge in the brain I have no idea but once they do, it's almost impossible to shift them. It's not even the same as ear-worming, where you hear a song or someone mentions the title and it infiltrates your head like an infection.

The songs that appear while fishing can come from anywhere and they can come from nowhere. All your casting, retrieving and, hopefully, catching are accompanied by an inner soundtrack that goes on all day long. It won't surprise anyone who has ever fished Willowgate that Bridge Over Troubled Water is usually first on my playlist when I pop in to visit the trout.

This fishery is a curious place. If you stand in the right spot and study it from a particular angle, what lies before you is a charming, attractive, decent-sized water – not far short of 10 acres – with enough different features to keep you interested, plenty of greenery provided by the trees down one side and the mighty River Tay rolling by on the other. You will have a range of wild birds for company and you might even spot a deer chancing a drink at the water's edge down the bottom end if no one is fishing there.

All lovely and scenic and rural, right? Yes, but only if you don't move from that spot and keep your fingers in your ears because an endless stream of cars, vans and trucks is thundering almost directly overhead on the busy Friarton Bridge that carries traffic in and out of Perth. That's not all though, because if you are a competition-class line chucker, you would be in danger of hooking a train on your back cast and having to dash to Perth station to ask for your flies back.

If that makes Willowgate sound urban and ugly, it is anything but. The traffic soon becomes a background rhythm and the occasional trains a blur because the quality of the fishing will quickly win you over and hold your attention.

Anyway, back to the soundtrack and I couldn't shake the Simon and Garfunkel classic for a good hour while trout rose and splashed but stubbornly ignored every dry fly I offered them – and a couple of wets into the bargain. Then I tried an old favourite stand-by up at the top end where the water narrows and my fortune – and the music in my head – changed almost instantly.

Foam Beetles are always worth a throw and so often prove to be a good bet for rousing trout and saving a blank when they are being fussy. I once saw a very good angler defy a blizzard-class caenis hatch on a muggy summer's evening to catch steadily on Beetles while all around him folk were tearing out their hair as well as those tiny bugs from their jackets.

First cast with the Beetle at Willowgate and within seconds it was fish on, even if it was fish off just as quickly. But at last some action and even though the pedants might tell me the spelling is different, the little DJ in the back of my head decided it was appropriate to bring on John, Paul, George and Ringo. Here Comes The Sun was first up but thankfully it didn't tempt the big yellow guy out from behind the cloud cover, though it did form the backing track for the first of a string of bruising rainbows.

Willowgate never fails to present a worthy challenge and once you've figured out what the fish are in the mood for, some excellent sport – and classic tunes – generally follow.

POSTSCRIPT: Willowgate has been one of my go-to venues for years because it's such a handy spot for a couple of hours fishing during regular visits to my daughter, who lives not far away. I have sharply contrasting memories of staring at an indicator on a sub-zero winter's morning while losing contact with my feet, and winkling out a few on Suspender Buzzers at the height of a sizzling summer's afternoon.

I can also remember failing miserably to teach my other daughter Lynn how to cast there then watching her out-catch me after one of the fishery guys set her up with a bung and a Millennium Bug, along with a guarantee it would work. There is always an easy-going atmosphere and almost always good sport to match.

Another great Willowgate memory was when I mentioned the Beatles song in my column and my puntastic pals on the paper decided we couldn't let the opportunity pass without compiling a list of fishing-related Fab Four songs. We finished up with enough for a whole record – The Whiting Album, of course. From memory, they included Twist and Trout, Maxwell's Silver Hammerhead, Drive My Carp, Stockie Racoon, Bleny Lane, Bungalow Brill and my headline – The Long and Wind-in Rod.

KINROSS & EASTER BALADO, SEPTEMBER 2015.
They might have been close neighbours, barely a mile and a few minutes apart, but I'd been told I wouldn't believe how different these two fisheries were – and that was exactly why I had to check out both of them. I did just that within a few days of each other in similar conditions and discovered my advance information had been correct. They

166

shared virtually nothing but a motorway exit.

Kinross was first up and I got a good feeling about the place right away. There are four waters set amidst lush parkland which belies the site's history as a sand and gravel quarry. Two of them are fly only with spinning and bait allowed on the others.

My big dilemma was whether to concentrate my efforts on getting to know one of them well or to keep on the move and at least check out all of them. I remember a similar reaction the first time I fished Forbes of Kingennie.

The first thing that struck me at Kinross was the friendly atmosphere, starting with the then fishery manager Neil Pozzi, who was happy to point me in the right direction. I was also impressed with how the regulars were quick to spot a newcomer and generously share tips on flies and hotspots.

Just a pity the trout weren't as forthcoming in the mild, muggy late afternoon and evening. The fish were there OK, they just weren't in the mood, or at least not interested in anything I was offering.

As the light faded, I had just about settled on a blank and a determination to return for another go when a trout I had stalked for about 10 minutes finally gave me a break. The fight from an exceptionally well-conditioned rainbow right at the death just about cancelled out the few hours of frustration that had gone before.

Fast forward 72 hours and I have to admit that I didn't get the same warm feeling about Easter Balado on first impression.

Sure, the tree-lined setting was pleasant enough but basically you are looking at a featureless, rectangular slab of water. The fact that large sections were choked with weed and much of the bankside was boggy didn't exactly endear me to the place.

My enthusiasm wasn't exactly brimming over then – until I discovered how damn good the actual fishing was, especially the top-of-the-water sport which is always going to get my vote. The trout, all of a good stamp, eagerly and consistently came up for Yellow Owls and F-Flies and once hooked, fought with the kind of no-rules energy of street brawlers.

Kinross v Easter Balado? One place that, for me anyway, came within a whisker of being the fishery that had everything but a fish, and the other the fishery with almost nothing to offer but fish.

POSTSCRIPT: It has always nagged at me that I didn't do Kinross justice because I tried to sample too much of it at once rather than concentrating on one of the waters and saving the others for another day.

That was a real pity because it's a place with genuine history as one of Scotland's original trout fisheries, if not the very first.

A good guy named Billy McFerren, who many people in the fishing world will know, once told me a nice story about it. He was out hunting and stumbled across Heatheryford – as it was called then – not long after it opened in the late 1980s. Anglers were spaced apart around a pond and he had never seen anything like it – fly fishing for trout in the winter.

The moment proved life-changing because Billy had been looking for a new project and went on to establish Lawfield, in Renfrewshire, another of the first wave of fly fisheries 30-odd years ago.

As for Easter Balado, it is no longer operating as a fishery but you never know, that may change in the future.

Chapter 13

Salmon-chanted evening

I AM haunted by the ghosts of two salmon for completely opposite reasons. One I caught and, increasingly over the years, wished I hadn't. The other I didn't catch but fervently wished I had. Yes, of course, we all lose fish, happens all the time. But of all the ones that have got away in my angling lifetime, that salmon is among the two or three I most regret which is a paradox because I have to make a confession here and it feels like heresy or sacrilege. But here goes. *I don't like salmon fishing very much.*

There, said it, and I will try to explain later which in itself will not be easy because even if they are never my go-to quarry, there is no denying the special grip that the king of

170

fish has on almost every game angler, me included.

Let's deal with the ghosts and I'll start with the regret over the one I did catch because that came first, about 30 years ago in fact, and even though it is distant in time, it left such a mark on me that I remember every detail.

I was living in Newton Stewart at the time, editor of the local newspaper, and I had just been converted to fly fishing after being a staunch bait and spinner devotee since childhood. I was shown the ropes by a brilliant bloke called Andy Johnstone, a printer on the paper who I still go back and fish with every year. I was the archetypal kid with a new toy and couldn't get enough of it, though I did all my learning and refining on the local angling association's excellent trout lochs, fearing salmon on the fly was a whole new level I wasn't ready to step up to.

Such was my total immersion that for a whole season I virtually ignored our club's jewel in the crown, the mighty River Cree. I guarantee that anyone who has ever visited Newton Stewart will have been unable to resist a snap of the picture postcard stone bridge under whose arches the river flows parallel to the main street.

Before I knew it, we were well into October and the season was in stoppage time with the ref looking at his watch. So for the last week and a bit, I spent every spare minute on the Cree, determined to get a salmon, though I lost my nerve and reverted to the spinning rod.

On the second last day, a big fish swam straight up to a bunch of worms that I had left hanging in the current just down from my riverside flat. Heart thumping, I watched it open its jaws, clamp its gob over my bait and turn. I did everything by the book, waited a couple of seconds till I felt it, then lifted into it. Perfect. Except there was nothing there and I felt robbed. But in the words of Uncle Tony, my favourite gangster, what you gonna do? I was convinced my opportunity had come and gone for another year.

Then it was the final day of the season, last chance saloon, and the fishing gods were against me. It was a Friday, the day we went to press, but there was a production problem and I had to work through lunch rather than nipping out for an hour in the middle of the day. No problem, I'd just finish early. But then a local councillor, who campaigned about stuff like dog poo on pavements and loved seeing his name in print, dropped by late in the afternoon and even when I stood up, put my jacket on and turned the office light off, refused to take the hint and carried on bending my ear about some small town trivia.

I didn't get on to the river till gone five, barely a couple of hours of precious daylight left. I concentrated on the bank where I'd lost the fish the previous day but as it began to get dark and a mist settled in, I gave way to a trio of step-and-cast fly fishers. I crossed the pretty bridge back to the main street and headed for a gap in the wall opposite the fire station where I knew I could get a cast if no one else had thought of it first. It would also give me the advantage of a street light at my back so I could see what I was doing for a little longer.

By the back of eight, it was not only completely dark but the mist had thickened and was sitting on the water. It was time to raise the white flag and call it quits. But then I heard a guy on the opposite bank say, simply, *Yes*. I squinted through the murk and caught the odd ghostly glimpse of him on the move, following the fish up river, rod straining,

172

and every so often I heard the splash of the salmon as it fought for its life. This went on for what seemed an age but was probably less than five minutes. From the vague outlines I could make out, the splashes were getting closer to the bank, signalling that the battle was almost over.

Suddenly there was a crack like a dry twig snapping, then silence for a moment before a stream of curses bellowed from across the river. Poor sod, whoever he is, I thought. What a way that would have been to finish the season.

I could almost feel the rage and the frustration floating over from the other side and stood there, silently commiserating, for maybe a minute until I felt my own rod, gripped loosely in my right hand, turn away from me slightly. So caught up was I in the action elsewhere that I hadn't given a thought to my own line still being out. Now that I was paying attention again, I assumed it had drifted into the bank and my hook was caught on the wall somewhere downstream.

Then I realised the line was straightening and my rod tip was moving slowly but steadily in the other direction towards the middle of the river. Surely not? I tightened up carefully until I felt the solid connection and hit it, firmly but not violently. Now there was no doubt. Fish on, a salmon, right on the whistle.

But here's the thing, it didn't respond properly. The resistance was half-hearted at best, like it was going through the motions. The fish made one strong, ponderous run but after that it felt like I was playing the weight of it against the current.

I'll get this over with quickly because it feels awkward

writing it in this more enlightened age, but I killed it and stuck it head first into my bag for the short walk home. It was a bright, fresh fish, somewhere around the mid-teens, which should have been the perfect closing day prize. But even from the start, it didn't feel right.

The triumphant production back in the flat, with close friends gathered around the kitchen table, was tainted. Same for the back slaps from a couple of fellow club members next morning. Truth is, I never felt good about that fish and it still niggles at me from time to time.

For a small town where it was almost impossible to keep your business under wraps, it was a surprise that no one revealed themselves or was identified as having dropped a good salmon on the last night of the season. There were several credible theories – embarrassment at losing the fish, someone chancing their arm without a permit under cover of darkness, a visitor with a day ticket.

I tried hard to convince myself it just wasn't feasible that a salmon would knacker itself fighting an angler to within an inch if its life, then grab a worm sandwich as an encore. But I couldn't get the lack of fight out of my head. No one takes on a salmon and forgets the bursts of sheer unbridled power and the grim, bloody-minded determination. I will never know for certain, of course, but equally I will never shake off the suspicion that I caught someone else's fish.

There was no doubt about the salmon that forms the other half of the double haunting. That was definitely my fish from the moment I hooked it until it broke my heart and dropped me to my knees.

Actually, I should rewind 24 hours because the events of the day before are relevant, right from the surreal start which summed up perfectly how fishing is our escape tunnel.

My mate Alan and I had decided to switch our annual Hebridean pilgrimage from brown trout in May to a crack at the back-end salmon in September. I'd had to work a couple of extra days so the plan was that he would drive up with the gear and I would catch the first morning flight on an old windy-up prop plane to join him halfway through the week.

Sounds simple when you write it down but I slept through the alarm after a breaking story kept me late on the paper the night before. Then I got caught in motorway work traffic, hopped from one foot to the other as I endured the painful crawl through security, bolted to the furthest away gate at Glasgow Airport while my name was called out on the PA system and breathlessly threw myself on to the Stornoway plane as they were wheeling the steps away.

Less than an hour and a half later, I was hiking with rod in hand along a rough, steep track to the upper river on the exclusive Morsgail estate on Lewis, where we'd blagged a day's sport thanks to the island contacts built up over the years. It was a whirlwind leap from motorway madness to proper wilderness.

Morsgail was huge fun, not least because the first part of the day was basically trout fishing for salmon – a narrow, peaty burn, ten-foot six weight and a couple of Size 12 flies cast from well back, as we stayed hidden among the gorse. I disturbed one salmon which kissed an Orange Muddler without making proper contact then had a brace of decent-sized, dusky brownies which thrashed about angrily with nowhere to run.

Their sea trout cousins were first to make an appearance when the estate ghillie rowed us out on the small but perfectly formed Morsgail Loch in the afternoon.

We had drifted almost the full half mile from top to bottom of the loch when I was thumped by a salmon – definitely not the best time to discover the drag on my reel wasn't working. It quickly locked up tight and the fish departed with a ping.

Sure, I could delve deep for reasonable excuses. The start of the day, from leaving my house back on the mainland to meeting the ghillie, had been such a manic rush that there had not been a second to check my gear. Or perhaps my faithful old Greys reel had been on the point of packing in and the jolt from the fish had sealed the deal. But no, losing a salmon like that was amateurish and rightly, I felt embarrassed, even more so since I had left my two spare reels in the car.

I made some sort of amends shortly afterwards when the only salmon of the day also fell to my Orange Muddler and I managed to improvise by controlling the line in and out of the knackered reel by hand until I got it under control. It wasn't a big fish by any means – around 6lb – but what it lacked in size it made up for in fighting spirit and it was a bonus end to the day that I scarcely deserved.

So, when we pitched up on another river the next day, I was desperate to prove, to myself more than anything, that I could do things properly, take a salmon the right way without making a pig's rear end of it.

It was a modest kind of river, curling through desolate country, again requiring only trout gear but capable of producing powerful fish in good numbers. As we set out, I got a taste of the kind of Hebridean wisdom that is born of living close to nature, close to the land and water, and passed down through the generations.

"Don't rush yourselves, boys," said the estate manager. "Have some casting practice, enjoy your lunch in the hut on the beat, because nothing's going to happen till four o' clock."

I shrugged it off as some kind of folksy superstition – *ne'er cast a cloot* and all that – but I should have known better. None of the three of us – Alan, our island pal Alastair, or me – had a serious touch for most of the day, discounting a posse of small trout and one dubious knock I had just before lunch which wasn't worth writing home about.

We had made a long, sweeping pool our base and went off exploring in both directions and for various distances before I drifted back there at around ten to four and met the estate boss, who had parked up at the roadside 20 minutes away and wandered over. I chatted to him for five minutes and had just got my fly back in the water when Alastair appeared from upstream, grinning and holding up his phone.

"I just got a fish," he called, but before he was close enough to show us the pic, his mobile rang and we heard him talking, to Alan as it turned out. "Ah, grand, what size? Hang on, there's Mike into one just now. Good fish by the looks of it."

I was, and it was. I don't think I have ever been hit harder by a fish, like a full-blooded smack on the head that comes out of nowhere and it was difficult to avoid the cliché about buses all turning up at once.

I don't want to be big-headed here but I can look back, hand on heart, and know that I did everything right that day. With plenty of space to run in the broad sweep of the pool, I gave the fish its head but kept just enough pressure on all the way so that I was always in control. When it wanted line, I made the fish earn it. When it stopped to recharge its batteries, I recovered line. At times the runs were relentless and a good third of my rod was in the water but little by little, I was gaining ground until, finally, it began to tire and I was able to slide it towards me, bit at a time.

The estate manager volunteered to land it and, grabbing the net, slid off the bank and into the shallows. The salmon made a couple of final bursts but I sensed it was ready and began walking backwards, the rod straight up in the air, estate boss ready to lift the net. I wasn't sure how close he was but suddenly all pressure was released and I thought it was because he had taken the weight from me. Until I saw his face.

Maybe we make too much of these things. It's only a fish after all. But I felt desolate, unable to comprehend the loss. I sank to my knees and neither of the two others could look at me. There would be a fatal accident inquiry, of course. There always is. But right at that moment, I couldn't face it and trudged off down the pool, found a boulder and sat down, my knees next to my ears.

However much I tried to rationalise it, however much the other guys insisted I'd done everything right and that sometimes these things just happen with no explanation, I never really got over that fish. After the farcical performance of the previous day, this had felt like redemption but turned into a punch-in-the-guts experience

178

I have never quite managed to erase.

Talking of fish I've tried and failed to forget, there was also the one on the Dee that finally forced me to admit a feeling that I had been trying to suppress – that I was increasingly finding the pursuit of salmon less than thrilling at best, a complete turn-off at worst.

I had been so looking forward to fishing this particular beat of the Dee since being shown it during the close season by a pal of the ghillie. He had introduced me to some of the very different pools and pointed out a few likely lies which I tucked away for future reference.

I wanted to savour this session so I got there good and early, day ticket bought at the bailiff's cottage and tucked in my back pocket. I parked up in the lay-by near the bridge and as this was in the Spring – late March or early April from memory – I started at the very top of the beat armed with intermediate line and a couple of the river's classics, a Dee Monkey and Ally's Shrimp.

Slowly, methodically, I edged my way down the entire length of the beat – probably close to two miles. I was taking my time because there was no one directly behind to push me on. Step-cast, step-cast, step-cast. I saw one fish splash a couple of times, once ahead to my left then again just off my right shoulder, but I touched nothing other than a baby brown trout with eyes bigger than its belly. I picked away at it, concentration full-on, slowing down on the lazy bend when I sensed I was running out of water.

After a while, it felt more like work than play but I kept telling myself, it's salmon, this is how it goes. You've got to pay your dues but eventually you'll get your reward. Might not even be today but sooner or later…

There was a sandbank near the end of the beat where I sat on a stump of wood and, over my sandwiches and flask soup, seriously wondered if I should hike back to the car and switch to trout gear or even just cut my losses and head to a loch for the afternoon so I could be reminded what it was like to feel something pulling my line. I gave myself a shake and told myself to stop whining, get a grip, march back up to the start, do not collect £200 for passing Go, and do it all again.

It's funny how a salmon beat can seem so much longer when you are not fishing. Had I really covered all that water? Yes, there was the little bay with the shingle. The stretch with the overhanging trees where I'd hooked the crisp poke ditched by one of my less environmentally alert brethren. The sheer bank where I'd underestimated the strength of the current and had to plant myself firmly until I got my balance.

I was almost back at the bridge when I saw another angler edge through the narrow opening next to the parapet on the main road. He spotted me and began hurrying towards the water, so I eased my pace and waved my hand in a slow-down motion, the way you gesture to oncoming drivers when they're heading towards an obstruction in the road or a speed trap. I had already decided I might only cover half the beat this time so I was in no rush. I would let him get a good bit ahead before slipping in behind him.

You can probably guess what comes next. He had a couple of medium casts while he pulled line out and on his second full-length throw, his rod bent into a fish. He played it like a pro, declined my offer to net it for him, but did rub salt in the wound by passing me his silver digital camera to

180

do the honours before he carefully sent back a nice springer of maybe 11lb to continue its journey.

Of course, the decent human being in me was magnanimous, genuinely pleased for him. But there was part of me that couldn't help thinking, *Oi, Johnny come lately, that was my fish. I've put in the hours, the effort, and you swan in here and lift it from right under my nose. If you'd arrived five minutes later, it might have been me in the right place at the right time.*

It was scant consolation to discover there wasn't even something different he had done that I could learn from. Intermediate line and an Ally's Shrimp. Snap.

On the drive back down to Glasgow, I cursed the timeslip that might – just might – have made all the difference. That was the moment when I came to the conclusion that I'm not really the biggest fan of salmon fishing. Almost a full day on one of Scotland's classic salmon rivers and I couldn't honestly say I'd had a good time.

Please note, I am not saying for a minute that I don't enjoy catching salmon because I've yet to find anything to compare. It's just all the other stuff before you get to the catching – the repetitive slog, the lack of logic, the arbitrary outcome – that leaves me cold. Don't get me wrong, I am happy to acknowledge the shortcomings are all mine and that if I stuck at it, I would get better at it. Actually, the real problem is that I probably don't believe that, at least the last bit.

Thing is, with trout fishing, I feel I can usually go some way to affecting the outcome. I can try to solve problems. I can take clues from the time of year, the temperature, the light, the wind, the depth, the location.

Now, some or all of that might apply to salmon as well and I'm just too thick to grasp it but it feels too much like a game of chance, like waiting for the accidental combination of putting your fly in front of the one fish which just happens to be there and reacts by biting it. Don't forget, this is a fish that doesn't eat in fresh water anyway so it doesn't have a reason to bite your fly.

Sorry, but it just feels like too much time invested on a lottery – and a bizarre pastime where sometimes you catch the other guy's fish and other times, he catches yours.

Chapter 14

Walking on Finn ice

T has been my worst, ingrained fear since we arrived in this land of snow and ice – and it has just happened. Three of us are walking across the frozen lake, side by side, in the blackest darkness I have ever been enveloped by, the beams of our head-torches dancing on the smooth crust in front of us. I am in the middle with Pasi, our driver and host, on my right. Janne, the fishing guide, is on my left. I have only known these guys a matter of hours but already we're chatting and laughing away like old buddies, the way fishing folk often do. I think this happens because anglers are united by a passion that gives us immediate common ground and countless stories to swap.

Anyway, the atmosphere is so convivial that you can

almost – but not quite – forget how damn cold it is. Then, instantly and without any warning, Janne disappears. That primeval dread I'd been battling – of the ice cracking and swallowing a person – has come true. Instinctively, I reach for…

But no, let's leave it there for now. This, in writers' world, is what we call a cliffhanger – the setting up of a tense moment in the narrative that teases the reader and leaves them wanting more.

So sorry, but you'll have to wait a few minutes to discover Janne's fate while I fill you in on where this happened and why I was there, in a fishing sense of course. But hey, you already know this isn't the most serious fishing book you've ever read in your life, so surely he's not really going to die?

Or does he?

You'll just have to wait and see.

Talking of impending death, I must admit to harbouring a few suspicions when my family unveiled a surprise present for a special birthday. Which special birthday? Well, if you've seen the mugshot that goes alongside my newspaper column, your first thought might have been that you didn't even know George Clooney was into fishing. Your second thought, once you'd looked a little more carefully, was probably, *that can't be Mike 40 already.* Sadly, not that birthday. Try a bit higher. No, higher still.

Now, I'd be lying if I said I wasn't at least half expecting some kind of fishing trip as a birthday gift from my family. It's my thing, what I love doing and when it comes to gifts these days, we tend to give each other events, concert tickets, short breaks and so on, rather than more stuff.

FISHING IN THE SUN

There I was then, trying to second-guess them. Thinking, Florida Keys for the bonefish, maybe the Caribbean for tarpon, Africa for any number of exotic species. What I'd never considered was opening the card with the big six-o on the front to find a home-made voucher with a still on the cover from Grumpy Old Men – the original movie with Jack Lemmon and Walter Matthau, not the telly whinge-fest – and an invite to a week's ice fishing in Finland.

Come on, you can't blame me for momentarily wondering if there was an ulterior motive. Had my wife and kids heard something about the value of the house and my pension – their inheritance – that I hadn't? Bear in mind, this was just a couple of years after only the skill of heart surgeons had kept me in the land of the living. What better way to finish off someone with a dodgy, patched-up ticker than despatching them on a fishing trip to a sub-zero wasteland?

Once I convinced myself they weren't trying to get rid of me, the excitement set in and it turned into one of the great adventures of my life. Mind you, there were a couple of humps to get over before I could properly appreciate my birthday present, not least my missus setting our stopover hotel in Manchester on fire trying to get the shoddy toaster to work at breakfast.

Our epic journey of, quite literally, planes, trains and automobiles, was almost at an end before the next big scare. We had been picked up by the aforementioned Pasi at the railway station in the town of Mikkeli after a two-and-a-half hour train journey from Helsinki and now he was driving us deep into Finland's Lakeland. It was close to midnight and having been travelling since early morning, we wanted

185

nothing more than to get to our destination, collapse and start afresh next morning.

I had just about resigned myself to the sensation of being driven along snow-packed roads at high speed when our 4X4 suddenly careered off the road and down a tree-covered verge. Convinced Pasi had skidded off the highway, a jolt of panic shot through me and I instinctively reached out for my wife and prepared to lose our faces in airbags. But next thing I knew, we were back on the road – and heading for the middle of a lake. By road, I mean ice road.

There are some things in life you think you'll never get used to and for me, being driven across a frozen expanse of water is one of them. Not even the cars and trucks and snow ploughs routinely charging up and down the ice roads made me feel any better about the idea.

But this is the winter wonderland of Finland and the rules you've lived by all your days don't apply here so you have no choice but to learn to roll with it. It makes perfect sense, of course. When the lakes are frozen for nearly half the year, why drive all the way round them when you can save time and fuel by cutting straight across. Just don't expect me to get used to it.

Our base was a cosy wooden cabin on the edge of Lake Soukkio, as warm and comfy as it was well equipped, though with temperatures averaging 16 below zero, we never worked up the courage to try out the sauna. It is in the heart of the Finnish Lakeland, a vast wilderness dotted with thousands of bodies of water enclosed in dense pine forests, all frozen for five months at a time.

It takes a bit of adapting to, the notion that everywhere

you look is covered in snow – and that it's here to stay. There is a stillness and peaceful beauty to it all as shades of silver and grey sparkle in the air and shimmer through the trees. At those times when the weak sun was hidden, it felt like living in a black and white photo.

But enough of the picture postcard stuff, I was here to fish and once wrapped in multiple layers of thermals and boots that came with a claim that they were Arctic-proof, I soon found myself screwing up my eyes trying to spot a tiny red flag in a blizzard. The whipped-up snow was stinging my cheeks but I shrugged it off because I had a bite and as all anglers will testify, there is nothing that helps you forget adverse conditions like knowing there's a fish on. Carefully I lifted the polystyrene board covering the hole in the ice and tried feeling with my semi-numb fingers for the pike throbbing on the line.

Flag? Polystyrene board? Yes, this is fishing but not as we know it. This is going back to Primary One – strike that, it's more like nursery school – because any angling knowledge and skill that I had managed to pick up over the years counted for nothing.

For starters, I mostly fished for a week without touching a rod, unless you count a contraption shaped like a drumstick with a reel attached. It was an extraordinary insight into an approach to our sport that is a world away from what we do. In the first 24 hours alone, I was shown half a dozen fishing techniques, all born out of a climate that sees the country snowbound and the lakes frozen from November to April.

There is no one better to introduce you to Finland's fishing dark arts than expert guide Janne Parviainen.

Having fished since he was in nappies, he packed in an engineering job to make a career out of his real love. Watching and listening to him in action, you quickly figure out he is earning a living from what he would be doing anyway.

First up was catching bait fish a hundred metres out from our lakeside cabin. This turned out to be the closest to any methods I was familiar with. After drilling a hole in the 60cm ice – two feet in old money – we used a flimsy plastic line holder to pull up little perch and roach on dyed-pink maggot, or fly-worm as Janne called it.

Looking back, I was never happier during the whole trip than when I was perched on a stool in front of the little hole, line between my fingers, waiting for something to nibble at my bait – a throwback to catching minnows with thread and the head of a worm in a public park in Glasgow before I started school.

The Finns don't share our sensitivities or squeamishness about live bait so these fish go straight back under the ice as helpless prey for bigger perch, zander and pike.

For the bigger fish, Janne first demonstrated the centuries-old traditional set-up – line suspended from a thick branch laid across a hole with another forked stick holding it in place. You can't help but fall in love with the technique for its sheer simplicity. The modern equivalent – that polystyrene board with a spool of line and handle attached to the underside – got me my first pike of the trip, a jack of a couple of pounds.

Don't forget, you are doing all of this at temperatures most of us will never have encountered. Sensibly, you have plenty of hot drink breaks between shortish bursts of fishing.

Talking of the weather, I have lived in Scotland for most of my life so it goes without saying that I've fished in severe conditions aplenty. But nothing had prepared me for constant double figures below zero with a fierce blizzard slicing my face like fresh razor blades.

Interestingly though, the body adapts remarkably quickly. After our opening day minus-16 – as if Finland was trying to see what we were made of – it was a mere 11 below the day after and I found myself thinking, *Oh, that's not so bad. Quite mild, in fact.*

All the same, I've got to admit there is something very civilised about eating sizzling, spicy local sausages off an indoor barbecue, washed down with industrial-strength coffee, then going back out to find a biting fish has triggered my red indicator flag. That I could definitely get used to.

After that, we were off to check the ice nets and it's hard enough just getting your head round how this system of ropes and pulleys works under a solid, frozen surface. That produced the biggest fish of our stay – a pike of around 20lb so bright and glistening it looked like it was made from shiny plastic. There were numerous jacks and zander plus a few bream which were scathingly tossed into a pile to be mashed up for dog food.

By this point, my head was spinning with the array of species and methods – all the flags and nets and set lines and boards. But even if it's the kind of fishing that seems completely alien, you run with it because you realise that if you want to catch, you develop ways to do it according to the conditions and the environment. I was so caught up in all of this that I hadn't given a single thought to my favourite species, trout, and my go-to way of catching them, on the fly. My focus was entirely on trying to take in and learn what was in front of me.

But then I got a brilliant, unexpected opportunity and it was down to the thoughtfulness that we encountered every step of the way during our stay in Finland. You know, the little kindnesses that restore your faith in humanity, like the teenagers who put down their phones and leapt out of their seats to help us get our cases from the racks at our train station, and the gracious Finnair lady at Helsinki Airport, who ripped up the random boarding cards the check-in machine kept spitting out and sorted seats together for the flight home.

I'm hard pushed to think of a friendlier or more helpful bunch of people I have ever encountered – with the possible exception of the Japanese. It's as if, at some point, the Finns have held a national conversation and decided, *Look, life is tough and the winters are harsh so why don't we all try to get along and look out for each other.*

This gentle, thoughtful spirit translated to my fishing trip by way of an invitation to an exclusive trout paradise. During one conversation with Pasi and Janne, they quizzed me about the kind of fishing I did in Scotland and my answer was mainly about trout and flies. As far as I was concerned, it was no more than a casual chat.

I was already in bed when my mobile buzzed just before midnight. It was Pasi.

"Sorry to call you so late. If you would like to go to a trout fishery, I'll pick you up at seven."

Now, here is a lesson that I am happy to pass on. If you ever happen to find yourself in Finland and someone offers to take you to a trout fishery, do not expect to be targeting stocked rainbows on a small stillwater.

I found myself spending the morning at Lasakoski, a kind of sporting estate in the middle of nowhere with a fabulous river system and wild brown trout haven at its heart. I had to shove my way through waist-high snow drifts and break ice floes to wade into a wide, slow stretch for a couple of dozen casts. In truth, it was far too early in the year for the resident fish but it was worth it just for a look at the possibilities and potential.

I was also fortunate enough to meet another absolute gem of a fishing character in Matti Huitila, host at Lasakoski. He was kind enough to open up specially a few weeks early and give me a guided tour of the river, lodge and cabins before kitting me out with waders and fly gear. Apart from showing me some dreamy looking stretches that screamed out TROUT in two separate river channels, he was rightly proud of a network of streams and man-made backwaters where artificial spawning beds had been built to help along the next generation.

I have two particular memories that stand out from that delightful morning at Lasakoski. The first was discussing flies with Matti over mugs of muddy, caffeine-heavy coffee before heading for the river. As he went off for refills, he gave me his fly box to look through and for a few moments I was convinced he'd either given me the wrong one by mistake or else our target species had got lost in translation. I was looking at rows of salmon lures, surely? But no, these were match-the-hatch flies to represent the diet of giant bugs which packs super-strength muscle on to the brown trout.

191

Matti has fished rivers on our east coast and as I gazed in awe at these huge trout flies, he laughed and, in a passable attempt at an Aberdeen accent, said: "Och, you Scots and yer wee flees."

My other memory, not so funny – or at least not deliberately funny – came when Pasi lost control of his brand new drone while trying to film me casting and could only watch it dive into a deep, fast run. It was eventually retrieved and I had to make a serious effort to keep my face straight on the drive back to base as my miserable new mate kept shaking his head and muttering about a "helicopter crash".

The fly-fishing interlude aside, I spent almost all of the daylight hours on the frozen lake. When I wasn't fishing, I was either being towed across the expanse with my wife on a husky safari, whizzing around on, and frequently falling off, a fat-tyred bike, or trying a Kick-Sled which pretty much does what it says on the tin – think skateboard without the wheels. All that was courtesy of Rock and Lake Holidays and if you think it sounds like child's play, you'd be right and I make no apologies. Sixty going on six? That'll do for me. Mind you, it's chilly child's play, though saying yet again that it's cold is a bit like admitting Scotland gets a little rain.

Yes, all great fun on the lake but none of that had quite sealed my trust in the ice by the time I went out night-fishing with Janne and Pasi. We drove several miles across another water, Lake Kyyvesi, in search of what was a new species for me, the burbot. It's a sort of freshwater ling, now extinct in the UK but so numerous in the Middle Ages that they were used as pigswill. A shy creature which emerges under cover of darkness, it is sought after and considered a delicacy in Finland.

The burbot gave me an insight into Finnish humour because Janne and Pasi took great delight in telling me repeatedly that these fish were like teenagers – inactive all day before they liven up at dusk and turn predatory by night.

Without the watery sun to offer even the illusion of a tiny bit of warmth, the conditions that night were far and away the coldest I have ever fished in. The temperature was touching 20 below and I swear I could feel the strengthening wind drive holes into my brain like tent pegs.

The guys, turning serious for a moment, explained to me that the prospect of hypothermia was very real so the strict rule was 20-25 minutes fishing at a time max with breaks back in the 4x4 to thaw out. Otherwise, Janne warned in his scarily matter-of-fact tone, there was a fair chance we would, er, die. He also warned me against playing the macho card if I felt I couldn't stick it out that long – and told me to bear in mind they had both been coping with Finnish winters their whole lives and were used to it.

It took less than five minutes to realise he had not been exaggerating. I could not stop the violent shivering in every part of my body and I actually felt numb inside my skull by the time Pasi signalled we should make our first trek back to the wagon, about 100 yards away.

So, there I was, in the middle of our freezing but merry band as we followed the circles of light from our headlamps. I was nodding at one of Janne's stories when suddenly there was silence and he was no longer walking beside me. He had disappeared. Horror-struck, my breath caught in my throat as he plunged downwards through the cracked crust. Through nothing more than reflex, I reached out and made a grab for his arm, determined to cling on and stop him being trapped in a tomb of ice. But the momentum of his weight and the speed of his descent was too much and he slipped from my grasp. I didn't have time to take it in properly but I knew I was living the nightmare that had haunted me since I first set foot on the ice.

Then, just as suddenly, Janne was looking up at us with a grin and a thumbs up. I realised he wasn't sinking but standing up to his thighs in numbing water. He had crashed not through the ice but a long, snow-covered polystyrene board which had been placed over a fish trap. These traps – baited cages in, ironically, coffin-shaped trenches dug out of the ice – are perfectly legal but they are supposed to be marked with poles or flags and this one wasn't.

Remarkably, Janne recognised the handiwork and immediately started punching numbers on his mobile. It was one of those surreal, pinch-yourself, is-this-really-happening moments. There I was, way out of my comfort zone, night-blind on solid water not far from the Russian border, listening to a guy almost waist-deep in a giant slush puppy, berating someone with words I didn't understand but with an anger in his voice I certainly did. His tone shifted from rant to reasonable and finally, again amazingly, to friendly. The culprit was, ironically, the local fishing bailiff. He had come clean and apologised straight away before promising to come out with warning flags at first light. Yes, stable doors and horses.

Then came my second glimpse of Finnish humour. After Pasi and I had hauled Janne out of the pit, he looked at each of us in turn with his face an expressionless mask.

"OK gentlemen," he said in his perfect but heavily accented English, like he was in a Bond movie. "I have good news and I have bad news. The good news is that we can take any fish we want out of the trap for dinner.

"The bad news is..." and here he paused for effect. "There are two more of these traps between here and the car."

Chapter 15

Come fly with me

MY grandson Jimmy had his first birthday not so long ago but already he runs rings around me. He has developed the knack of distracting me with a cheeky grin or a cute new noise so he can sneak in and steal my iPhone. When he does, he flicks the screen with his tiny fingers as naturally as a child of my era lifting their first crayon.

Watching him doing it reminds me of the bewildering pace at which technology has advanced in little more than a generation and how developments that folk of my age think of as mind-blowing are already being taken for granted by small people who know no different.

We might think of fishing as a down to earth sport where

the basics never really change that much. Rod, reel, line, hook, bait. That's pretty much it. But, of course, we are not immune to the effects of the tech age, starting with the way folk buy their angling gear these days, i.e., online. You want new gear, the internet is the first place you look, even though, funnily enough, so many of us still get all mournful, nostalgic and seemingly surprised when yet another tackle shop shuts down. And where do we go to bemoan the latest closure? The internet, of course.

Thinking about online tackle shopping takes me on to smart phone apps which, I have to confess, I thought was short for appendages for a disturbingly long time. I shared that misconception with a well-known sports journalist I used to work with. He had already staked his place in newspaper folklore when mobiles first became standard issue for reporters. He stormed into his boss's office the morning after a big match, complaining that he had been unable to file his copy with the *stupid phone* he had been given. He declared he was refusing to use it ever again and tossed his television remote on to the sport editor's desk.

So, what has all this tech talk got to do with the practicalities of fishing? Well, when I tell you that my top trout fly the other day was an Electro-Head Mega Cruncher Starburst Twinkle Variant, you might begin to get the picture.

Thing is, I try to keep up with technology. I really do. I like flashy new stuff and it's not as if I feel ancient enough just yet to be using phrases like *new-fangled* and *in my young day.* At the time of writing, I am in my late forties. OK, that's very late forties as in 40-23. I still get genuinely excited and wide-eyed with wonder at the new tricks technology constantly teaches me but I have to confess that some of it is starting to slip past me and that is now translating into how I feel about trout flies.

Not that I'm blaming anyone for the never-ending stream of new wonder flies. I spent 40-odd years in newspapers so I'm more aware than most of the battle that print publications face to avoid being swept away by the tide of new media. Even as I was giving this book a last check for typos, I heard word of the sad demise of the Angler's Mail.

That emphasises my point. For fishing mags to survive, it's all about staying fresh, saying something new, looking modern and different. That definitely does not mean demonstrating how to tie a bog-standard Bibio for the 63rd time. The pressure never lets up to produce genuinely groundbreaking ideas or at the very least to modernise, improve, update and tweak the familiar.

Don't get me wrong. I am not being critical of this. Some of the creations that grace the magazine covers are irresistible and there is no doubt they will give you an extra edge.

My problem, and yes, I'm happy to acknowledge that it might be an age thing, is that I fear I have reached, or am at best approaching, saturation point. It's like, how much more new stuff is my brain willing or able to take on board? How many more new flies can I cope with?

At this point I stopped and told myself, you're writing a book so get off your butt, give the keyboard a rest and go do some proper research. If you want to write about the number of flies you have, don't guess, don't pluck a figure out of the air – go count them. OK, it would be an exaggeration to say it was like trying to count the grains of sand on a beach but it wasn't a trillion miles away.

There is a large wooden box somewhere that I used to think of as the Mother Ship. All the new flies would go in there, like the fresh crop of secondary school kids being gathered in the assembly hall before being assigned to their classes. So, there's the first job in the fly count – trying to locate the Mother Ship because I couldn't recall seeing it in years, never mind opening it. To my horror, when I finally located it in the bowels of the shed, it contained more than 1,400 pristine, brand new flies, all still patiently waiting for a posting.

I couldn't face embarrassing myself further so I emptied my fishing bag and created a mountain of stuffed-full boxes. But instead of counting, I just glanced over the contents and did rough estimates.

I'm talking about boxes for all the different categories of fly. The wets box, the dries box, the spare dries box, the buzzer box, the nymphs box, the worms box, the Daddies and Hoppers box, the Sedges and Beetles box, the dark-coloured lures box, the light-coloured lures box, the Bugs and Eggs box, the Blobs and Boobies box, the assorted boxes I've been gifted or won in charity auctions.

That's just the flies that are allegedly in use or at least close enough at hand to be called off the subs bench if required. I don't even want to think about all those drawers in the garden hut containing little clear poly bags stuffed with flies of all sizes and shapes which were either moved out of their boxes to make way for others or because they had "temporarily" fallen out of favour. They'll probably be further back in the drawer than the newish (probably up to five-year-old) ones that I either bought or have been sent by generous readers of my newspaper column to try out and haven't got round to sorting out yet.

I don't even want to guess at a figure, not least because many of them were bought and even at the very low estimate of 50p a fly, there is a small chance that my wife might read this and work out the number of extra trips to her favourite corner of Tenerife that she could have had.

I own so many flies that if I used a different one every 10 minutes when I'm out fishing, I wouldn't come close to getting through them all in what I have left of a lifetime.

But here's the kicker. Here's the real question. How many of those tens of thousands do I actually ever use? How many of those fancy new variants do I ever get round to trying?

A plain, shop-bought black Hopper has been catching me fish for as long as I've owned a fly rod and I can't think of a reason why it won't keep on catching me fish when I'm leaning on my Zimmer to cast. Does it really need some extra flash? Will the fish score it off their menu if it isn't reinvented with an injection of maribou?

Occasionally, I glance through musty old books from a century ago and read that anglers were catching on the same plain traditionals I still have in my box today. Hmm, if it ain't broke and all that.

Bottom line, I have my absolute go-to flies, my dependable first team squad and beyond the odd bit of occasional tinkering, that's how it will remain.

Which brings up the next riddle. The fly angler's version of the eternal chicken and egg question. We've all got flies we depend on, the ones we turn to more than all the others.

But do we rate them because they catch or do they catch because we rate them and therefore use them more than the rest?

As you'll have gathered, I am, or at least have been, a sucker for buying new flies. Whether it is online or in a tackle shop, it is almost certain that when I set out to buy half a dozen, I'd better be prepared to fork out for 50. Yes, I am a fully paid-up believer in – or victim of – the old cliché about flies being designed to catch anglers as much as fish. But what I am not so good at is turning the purchase into practical use.

If there is no obvious hatch on the go and a bit of blind prospecting is required, I stick to my old tried and trusted faithfuls. If it's wets for brownies, I'll almost always start with a Bibio, Kate McLaren, Black Pennel or Clan Chief. For rainbows, it's invariably dries. If they don't work, I'll turn to a Damsel, Fluff Cat, Diawl Bach or Montana Nymph.

Obvious picks and there's no rocket science involved. These are the flies I have consistently caught fish with and therefore the ones I look upon as my bankers. If they don't work, I'll usually change size or even line before pattern. But are they necessarily superior to the ones that languish in the box trip after trip? Or do they account for most of my fish simply because they're the ones most often on my cast?

To look at it from a different angle, there is a whole list of flies I don't particularly rate – and look away now if you're easily offended. The Butchers, Zulus, Dunkeld, Soldier Palmer and Peter Ross are flies that rarely feature for me. Logic and history tell me they are good flies. After all, they have starring roles in fishing lore and anglers much more talented than me have enough success with them to prove their worth.

Sure, I've caught the odd trout with them. The Soldier Palmer earned successive annual entries in my fishing log for catching the first brownie of the season two years in a row. My most vivid memory of the Dunkeld is of catching a non-stop procession of perch for 20 minutes at Loch Thom, near Greenock, on a bright May afternoon.

But the bottom line is, I don't give them a real chance so I have never learned to trust them. I will persevere with a Kate or a Pennel for hours on end but if a Butcher or a Peter Ross doesn't do the business in the first 10 minutes, it's already on borrowed time and heading back into the box.

The answer, if there really is one, comes down to faith and familiarity. It's a feeling that is hard to define but very definite – the knowledge that you are fishing with confidence.

I sometimes wonder if I would take a different view if I tied my own flies which takes us into a whole other area that I admit has given me more than a few troubling moments. I occasionally come across anglers who insist that you can't really call yourself a fly fisher unless you tie your own. Others will tell you that there are few better feelings than catching fish with a fly you have tied yourself and even more so if it is one of your own design.

That second claim I can understand more than the first. When I had a short-lived flirtation with the vice squad a few years ago, one of the first flies I had a go at – for its simplicity – was a Diawl Bach which ended up looking like a version that was trying but failing to recover from a particularly rough night out. But despite its bedraggled appearance, there was huge satisfaction when it attracted a few tentative offers if not actually a full-on take. It was as if the trout were saying, *Decent attempt, must try harder.*

But the notion that you are somehow not a complete fly angler unless you tie your own is not something I can buy into. I mean, no one thinks any less of golfers because they don't make their own tees or balls, do they?

No matter how often I rationalise it though, not tying my own flies is something that has bothered me in the past and still does from time to time. I suppose it's the idea that somehow you are being left out of a secret and that there is a whole mysterious level of fishing you are being excluded from – or are excluding yourself from.

I think my original reluctance to start tying was something to do with the idea that if I fancy a sandwich or a slice of toast, I don't feel the need to go out and buy a bread maker. Why bother messing about with all that yeasty stuff and figuring out gas marks on the oven when there's a huge choice of loaves on the supermarket shelves? Multigrain, wholemeal, rye, pumpkin seed, good old plain, mushroom and squid... OK, I made up that last one but you get the idea.

That was pretty much my view about tying my own flies. What was the point of all that time and effort when I could stroll into any old tackle shop and take my pick or else spend a lazy morning online – see above!

But then Mr Claus intervened one December 25 by delivering a basic kit which I felt obliged to have a play with so as not to offend the gift giver/daily meal provider. And yes, for a little while I landed myself with a new vice in more ways than one. Very quickly I found fly-tying every bit as absorbing and rewarding as I had been promised.

To any fellow novice, my best advice from limited – as in next-to-zero – experience is to get hold of a book that assumes you know absolutely zilch. I began working my way through Peter Gathercole's Fly Tying for Beginners, a real does-what-it-says-on-the-tin volume. It explains the basics in plain language along with idiot-proof – make that Kernan-proof – illustrations. Before you ask, no, I am not on commission.

A quick internet search will also turn up plenty of excellent YouTube clips – though you will find yourself constantly hitting the pause button and yelling *slow down mate* at the screen as the expert's hands become a blur. I came close to a couple of Chewin' the Fat style frenzies, especially when the thread snapped just at the last turn and I realised my book didn't have a fly-rescue chapter. But then came that magical moment when I held my own tiny creation between my fingers and realised, wow, that actually looks like it might just fool a fish – if it's short-sighted, famished and not too fussy.

After that first breakthrough, I might well have been persuaded to join the ranks of the committed fly-tiers. What stopped me was remembering that my wife, without a shadow of doubt, knows me much better than I do myself and that despite my protests every time she brings it up, I do have an obsessive streak.

It wouldn't have been enough for me to take it up as an occasional hobby. I wouldn't have been able to tie the odd fly to enhance my collection or when I wanted to try something different. I would have had to read every book on the subject I could lay my hands on, buy every piece of equipment I could find. I'd have quickly got on first-name terms with the Amazon delivery guy. Then, after I'd fought a losing battle for control of the spare room, I would have needed quotes from builders for an extension to house all the gear and give myself a place to learn and craft in peace.

Frankly, I don't have enough time in my life. I've got more important things to do, like go out fishing. That's not to say I won't ever come back to it but for now, I'm content to keep on buying flies when I need them or gratefully accept kind contributions from readers and fellow anglers.

What never changes, of course, is the need to look in all those boxes and choose the right fly for the occasion. I still can't help but envy those anglers who seem to know instantly and instinctively which fly to reach for.

Usually a bit of common sense and a quick scan of the conditions will point you in the right direction. The time of year, the light, the wind direction and strength, the temperature...all factors which will determine what the fish will be eating, if anything, and therefore what flies will give you the best chance of imitating their grub.

Trouble is, the trout stubbornly refuse to stick to the rules. Sometimes, in fact, I think they have an inbuilt detector that is designed to cut me down to size and remind me that more often than not, nature has the upper hand.

I remember once fishing with a pal on brown trout opening day at a loch deep in the Trossachs. We were there bright and early, raring to go and bouncing with all that new season enthusiasm. In truth, it was still a bit on the cold side as March 15 can so often be. (Actually, it was bloody freezing.) But we had come prepared with several layers of thermals, flasks of coffee, firelighters, frying pan, bacon and rolls.

Even through the extra padding and neoprenes, the water was icy cold but, dutifully, we stuck it out. Probably the fact we were a few hundred yards apart helped. Neither of us wanted to be first to wimp out after driving so far and so early. I started with my usual early season squad of Bibios and Black Pennels then went through the box but all in vain.

After a stop for lunch, it was back on and in the water and through the box all over again but still the trout refused to come out of hibernation. No one, it seemed, had remembered to tell them the season had started.

I reached the point where two things were becoming apparent. First, it was so cold in the late afternoon that I was losing touch with feet and fingers. Second, it didn't matter which fly or line I tried next, the fish were simply not for playing. In fact, I was having serious doubts as to whether there was anything alive in the place at all.

What the hell. Who cared about being first to raise the white flag? I trudged out of the water, perched myself on a rock at the edge and as this was in my bad old smoking days, lit up a B&H. When the cig was almost done, I flicked what was left of it just a few yards into the water and watched in a kind of disbelieving dream state as a hefty trout swirled at the cigarette butt, gulped it down and almost as quickly spat it back out.

Won't read that in too many match-the-hatch manuals.

Chapter 16

Thrill of the new

T'S probably something to do with the little kid that lives inside all of us that we get so excited by new things and in our case, new places to fish. Sure, it's always good to have a few, reliable waters that we know inside out – the runs, the hotspots, the tried and trusted methods that have worked before and will probably work again. To twist the old saying, familiarity breeds content.

Without question though, there is something special about fishing a new water, even if it is only new to us. It's about that very basic instinct to discover and explore, the thrill of the unknown. Will there be natural feeding, what will the quality of the fish be like, will there be plenty of space or will be it like combat fishing?

As you can imagine, writing a fishing column means I get the odd invitation to come and try places and write about them and as soon as I spot the word *new* in the details, I'm as good as there. So these were my impressions after visiting a bunch of trout fisheries while they were new, or at least, newish.

HADDOCKSTON, AUGUST 2009.

Honest Mike, you've got to try this place, my mate kept nagging me. But it's only another fishery, I said, what's the big deal? But he persisted. *I'm telling you, it really is something special, get along and give it a go.*

Finally, he wore me down so I got in touch with fishery owner Jackie McGough and agreed to take a run over to the little water, between Kilmacolm and Houston, one evening in late summer.

It took just 90 seconds to find out what all the fuss was about. That was when the express train left the station, tearing off line for fun and towing my Hopper towards the island. Across the water, Jackie grinned. He had raised his eyebrows at my choice of "brownie-proof' 3lb leader and warned I might need to go a fair bit stronger. Now, as I held on grimly, he might as well have a speech bubble coming out of his head saying, *Told you so.*

By that time, I was doubting my judgement too, amidst a fight that lasted five minutes but felt more like 10. A fine-looking specimen of a rainbow trout it was too – 5lb of solid muscle with a tail like a spade that at least partly explained its power. At the first opportunity, I made an excuse to sneak into the caravan that was serving as Jackie's temporary lodge. I was intent on finding the body-building supplement he must be feeding those trout – and I was prepared to return with a search warrant if necessary.

His explanation was more down to earth and logical. He told me: "Haddockston is spring fed, so they thrive on the natural life in the water."

Whatever the cause, I left that evening convinced that if there were harder fighting rainbows around in any small stillwater, you would go a long way to find them.

On a mild, calm night, they responded well to bushy dries at first then just as eagerly to Diawl Bachs left static. So yes, plenty of trout up for action and as if that wasn't enough of an attraction, they were living in a pretty little water set in lush seclusion in the heart of the Renfrewshire countryside.

I do stress the word *little* because there was no getting away from it – Haddockston was on the small side at barely three acres with not all of the bank fishable and I could well imagine it wouldn't take much to feel crowded.

Whatever the size of their accommodation, Jackie's trout were mobsters. They were greedy and bursting with aggression. If you had the audacity to hook one, you had to be prepared for a square go.

POSTSCRIPT: I became good pals with Jackie and fished Haddockston a few times after that. It was one of the most sheltered waters I'd come across so it became my haven in particularly foul weather. Just a few months after that initial visit, I returned in very different conditions of showers and gale force winds. After getting no response from dries and other small stuff, I started to hit fish with a black and green lure tweaked just below the surface. As ever, the Haddockston trout did not surrender without a fierce scrap. As a bonus, I got to feel good about myself by giving one of the lures to a drenched dad and son who had been fishing without success and used it to break their duck shortly afterwards.

The following February, I had an extraordinary day when I lost count of the fish that hungrily grabbed lures and wets after emerging from a long winter freeze. On the downside, I remember there were always niggles with a neighbour on the far bank and the place eventually closed as a commercial fishery.

At the time of writing, plans were underway to open it up again – neighbour problems permitting.

WOODBURN, MAY 2013.

Let's face it, anglers can't really move far without falling over a trout fishery. Loads of them serve up excellent sport in a pleasant setting and, more often than not, we get our strings pulled and go home happy. But if we're honest, there can be a bit of a same old same old feel after a while which inevitably leads to a longing to try something a bit different.

That was why I took to Woodburn so much on my first visit after it opened. Less than an hour from Glasgow, it managed to be in the middle of nowhere with a quality of fish anything but ordinary. Back then, I predicted a bright future for what was Scotland's newest trout fishery. It's nice to get something right now and again.

Ironically, what was so special on first impression was that the 12-acre water in the heart of the Campsies didn't look or feel like a commercial fishery at all – and I mean that in the best possible sense. Given it's a reservoir, you can forgive the fact that the water itself is a typical, fairly featureless bowl, but the dramatic backdrop of rugged hills quickly makes up for it.

A mile or so up the hill from the private Antermony Loch, there is a real wilderness feel around Woodburn, a desolate beauty which makes for the kind of venue where even before you start thinking of bothering the residents, it's simply a fine place to spend a day. It's a nice size too – plenty of room to breathe in the fresh air and do a bit of roaming, but not too daunting if you aren't used to the really large-scale waters.

Course, that stuff is all fine if you've got a knapsack on your back and love to go a-wandering, but what about the fishing? Happily, it was of a quality to match the surroundings.

It wasn't easy – or maybe that was just me! – and it required a bit of noggin-scratching and working out but that was fine. To me, a big part of the pleasure of fishing a new water in particular is the sense of achievement when you solve whatever puzzle it has placed in front of you and reap the rewards.

Woodburn has excellent water clarity and an abundance of rich feeding, so it was plain to see the top-grade trout wouldn't stay stockie-friendly for very long. Once located, they didn't half make their presence felt and refused to come easily or happily to the net.

The first I encountered didn't so much take my Daiwl Bach as hammer it before spitting it back out again. I was ill-prepared and far too slow to react but I didn't make the same mistake again.

I knew some double-figure brownies and rainbows had been added to the mix so there was always the chance of connecting with a brute. I didn't bump into any of the big beasts that day but there was enough fight in the series of 3lb-plus rainbows I tussled with to keep me happy.

POSTSCRIPT: This is one of those cases of time rushing away without realising it, which is sadly all too familiar the older you get. I was shocked when I checked back through my log books and realised my one and only visit to Woodburn was so many years ago.

My memory of that day is vivid – thinking how attractive Antermony looked despite the murk of wind and rain, fearing I'd taken a wrong turn as the rough track seemed to wind its way upwards forever, counting myself lucky that I'd brought a landing net with an extending handle when I saw the height of some of the fishing positions.

Woodburn's reputation has soared over the years and anyone who fishes the place raves about it. No question, it is my loss that I have not been back and I need to put that right before much more time slips away.

BROOMHILL, MARCH 2017.

Everyone knows the old saying about how good things come to those who wait, right? Well, I discovered where it originally comes from – the trout of Broomhill.

There are times when we just refuse to see sense and my first visit to the then newly opened trout water at this match fishery was a case in point.

The howling wind and torrential downpour should have been enough of a deterrent to stay indoors. But it had been a particularly foul spell of weather that was showing no signs of calming down and I hadn't been out for a few weeks so I decided I was going out fishing whatever the conditions chucked at me.

As decisions go, it wasn't the smartest I'd ever made and what clinched it was the mudbath that confronted me when I got there because the pond was so new, it was still in the process of being landscaped. I did think about getting straight back in the car and writing off the day but it had taken me long enough to find the place in darkest East Ayrshire. Besides, I had come to fish so what the hell.

As I picked my way round to the far bank to get the gale behind me, every step felt like wrenching my boot out of superglue. The tiny, remaining scrap of good sense in me dictated that I wasn't going to hang about too long.

But the hour or so I stuck it out for was enough time to hit a couple of solid trout on a Leggy Bloodworm and a third on my old pal, the WSW. I'd made my point, even if I'd got half-drowned in the process, and concluded that this new trout water hinted at good things to come.

April 2018.

I returned a year later, in very different conditions, to find that I had to wait just a little longer still to see what Broomhill was really all about. I eventually enjoyed a sensational spell but it came only after a bit of a slog – and left me with a pang of guilt because I had it all to myself.

Let me set the scene. I turned up at the fishery just after lunchtime to find a mass head-scratching session going on in one of those annoying, frustrating days of brassy light and a stiff, swirling breeze that couldn't make up its mind which direction it wanted to blow in. Sure, the odd fish had

213

been caught here and there – a monster reputedly among them – but generally it was slow going. Hardly anything was showing and, worse, there seemed to be no rhyme or reason to it.

Word around the water was that one angler had caught a rainbow on top with a dry while another had got a couple deep down on a Snake. One fish had supposedly been tempted by a Diawl, another on a bug under an indicator, yet another on a lure. In other words, one of those bitty days when the occasional fish was being caught but there was nothing to get a handle on, no method or depth working consistently and therefore worth concentrating on.

I fitted right in – one trout thrashed unconvincingly at a Suspender Buzzer on the third or fourth cast and an hour later, another nudged a Fluff Cat on a slow glass but that was it. The only consolation was getting to hear one of my all-time favourite fishing exchanges between two fellow strugglers.

Angler 1: "The fishing urny f*****g playing."

Angler 2: "Aye, scaly basturts."

So perhaps the general air of disappointment and puzzlement explains why the place virtually emptied bang on 5pm, as if an end of shift hooter had sounded that only I couldn't hear. I figured those who left had either been there longer than me and had had enough or just had better things to do on a Saturday evening.

I might well have followed them swiftly if I hadn't glimpsed something out of the corner of my eye. Was that actually a rise? Cue a wander down to the far corner, just in case. No one had been fishing in that spot and yes, there was another circle opening up or maybe just the same solitary trout again. But I glimpsed another one to my right, then a trout breaking the surface further down the bank. Within a few minutes, the water in that corner had basically exploded.

Out went a Size 16 Olive CDC as quickly as I could tie it on and it was on the surface less than three seconds before it was smashed by the first of Broomhill's beautifully conditioned rainbows. It's not just about looks though, as I quickly rediscovered these powerful, top-quality fish fight hard – and every last inch to the net.

Funny how one trout can make all the frustration and failure disappear instantly because what followed was a frantic, action-packed two hours as just about every cast to a rising fish sparked a response. I lost count when I hit double figures. Add all the drops and misses – plus time replacing ripped apart flies – and the result was a mad, magical streak.

In the end, a top day at a spacious and well-run fishery and proof again that the fat lady does indeed sing about trout.

POSTSCRIPT: In retrospect, it was probably a slice of good fortune that my first trip to the new trout pond at Broomhill was cut short by a mud-caked monsoon. Ordinarily, I'd be hard pushed to make two visits to the same trout fishery in less than a year. But there was enough promise in that first, brief session to make me want to see how it would fish on a better day.

My overall impression was of a bland-looking and obviously man-made four-acre pond which won't grace too many scenic Scotland calendars. But if what you want is unadulterated, hard-core fishing action, Broomhill delivers…and then some.

DRUMTASSIE, MAY 2018.

It was the attention to detail that first caught the eye at Drumtassie. I'm talking about the small but important features like wind shelters with lights and charger points, landing nets and rod holders at every platform, little bins on the back of the seats to avoid the bank turning into a carpet of discarded nylon. All elements that, to me, make Drumtassie the epitome of a modern trout fishery – and I mean that in a positive way.

There are some anglers who turn up their noses at obviously artificial ponds and prefer to trek to wild places for trout. No one would argue with them either because that is the essence of proper fishing. But there is a huge constituency of people who, for their own reasons, have different priorities, like convenience and easy access, a bite to eat halfway through their day and a captive audience of fish right there in front of them.

Drumtassie doesn't pretend to be something it isn't, like a remote, natural water – though its woodland location near Armadale, West Lothian, is pleasant enough. But it does cater exceptionally well for the angler who simply wants a good day's no-frills fishing, end of.

When I popped in, I could quickly see how that experience would be enhanced by the tidy surroundings, clean, well-appointed facilities and a front-of-house gem in Leeanne Aitchison with her stream of good cheer and encouragement. Of course, all the shelters and charging points and customer care in the world count for zero if the fishing isn't up to scratch.

Drumtassie seems to deliver on that front too because it has a range of well-planned factors that ensure the stockies stay in good nick and are up for a battle. A burn flowing in and out means that not only is the water constantly freshened up but the current brings in aquatic bugs and insect life. There are trees near enough to supply more natural feeding but not so close that they will have you looking over your shoulder before every cast.

The result is that if you prefer to use more traditional and/or imitative flies, they will work just as well as your Boobies and Blobs and flashy lures. On top of that, the ponds have been designed with ledges and a variety of depths so the fish can thrive more naturally.

I'm sure it's possible to rack up a big score at Drumtassie but if conditions are not perfect, you will have to work for your trout – which is exactly as it should be.

The day I was there, the fishing was hampered by a pesky, pulsating wind that couldn't make up its mind which direction it wanted to mess up your presentation with. The trout weren't showing en masse so it was a case of keeping a sharp eye out for the odd rising fish and intercepting its path. This was no non-stop fish fest but enough trout did respond to Yellow Owls and CDCs to keep the interest levels ticking over all day.

These trout knew how to fight too, like the one that pinched my point fly in a couple of inches of water while I was ginking up the dropper – and didn't stop till it had bolted 20 yards down the bank and blood was oozing from my index finger. Then there was the very big trout – no, it really was – that led me on a merry dance for seven or eight minutes before breaking me when it glimpsed the net and made a last, surging dash for freedom.

All great fun and when you're fighting trout this tough, what's not to enjoy? For a fishery that had been up and running for less than a year when I visited, there was a very good feeling about Drumtassie. Well worth a visit and I'm pretty sure that if you go once, you will be back.

POSTSCRIPT: Like many of today's modern trout fisheries, anglers will either love or hate Drumtassie. Thankfully, Leeanne and co have found enough devotees to see the place go from strength to strength and that is in no small measure down to the positive way they treat people. There is now a sizeable raft of anglers with busy lives and/or limited time who want nothing more than to step out of their cars, find a comfortable spot, catch some fish with minimum hassle, enjoy a hot filled roll and a cup of tea, catch a few more, then go home again.

Angling is the pleasure part of your life so it should be exactly what you want it to be. That is pretty much Drumtassie's mission statement.

Chapter 17

Grounded

F OR nearly three months in 2020, something happened that I – and most other anglers, I'm certain – never imagined we would see in our lifetimes. *We weren't allowed to go out fishing.*

Strictly speaking, there was some doubt about that which I will explain in a moment. But effectively, our sport was banned just as surely as so many other elements of our daily lives were curtailed, while the invisible killer that was Covid-19 wreaked havoc with society. Fishing folk responded in very different ways and I wrote about some of the reactions as we went along as part living history, part personal therapy.

These are just some of the random scenes from the

lockdown.

MARCH 25-26. *Playing politics.*

AS the lockdown turned from days into weeks then into months, I often wondered how many anglers were aware that they could have fished their way right through it if only they had listened carefully to our political masters. I told readers of my column exactly that after a crazy, two-day dance that convinced me the handling of the restrictions was never going to be straightforward.

This goes back to the start, the Monday when first Boris, then Nicola, told us we were all grounded. The day after, there was understandable confusion about all aspects of the lockdown, fishing included. Anglers were bickering with each other online, quoting so-called facts that were not facts at all, about whether or not they could go out fishing. I decided it was my job, as a fishing writer for Scotland's biggest-selling newspaper, to get a definitive ruling.

Next day, the Wednesday, I asked a highly respected political journalist to get an answer straight from the horse's mouth. I still hold to the primary school lesson that the shortest distance between two points is a straight line so we fixed on the simplest possible question. *Is fishing allowed?* Dead easy, right?

What followed will give you an insider's glimpse into how the process between politicians and journalists works and the hoops that sometimes require to be jumped through to produce the simple line you will see in stories every day…*A Government spokesman said: "Blah blah blah."*

It took an hour and 40 minutes to get an initial answer which wasn't an answer at all but a paragraph lifted from

220

the SANA website saying going fishing did not count as essential travel.

My journalist pal batted it straight back, saying thanks, but what is the Scottish Government's own take on it? Another hour and a bit then a press officer sent a line from their own official guidelines about only going out for essential reasons including exercise once a day, with no mention of fishing.

My former colleague was, naturally, busy on the bigger political picture so didn't report back to me until that night when I told him that the Government's vague response was exactly what anglers were arguing about. He agreed that people needed straight answers and promised to try again next day.

He did and got a slightly expanded version of the previous day's answer about exercising once a day and was referred to the SANA website. He pushed back again, saying that didn't answer the question and added: "Please can we request some clear advice? We simply want to know if angling is permitted – from the government's point of view."

When that was met with silence, he told me: "This is madness. I've tweeted about it – maybe that will get their fingers out."

His tweet, at 4.25pm on the Thursday after lockdown, said: "Trying to get answer from Scot Gov about whether anglers are allowed to go fishing as daily exercise (debate is raging among anglers). Like nailing down jelly. For some reason Scot Gov won't clarify. Keep referring me to ambiguous statements by outside bodies. Really odd."

It did get their fingers out and 15 minutes later, my

persistent ex-colleague passed on their response.

"A Scottish Government spokesman told me that if anglers can walk to a nearby river and fit fishing into their daily hour of exercise, while maintaining social distancing, then it would be OK. People should not be getting in vehicles/journeying to go fishing, though."

So, there it was. After all that toing and froing, the official thumbs up to fishing, albeit within very strict limitations. I mean, how many people go out fishing for an hour, including walking time? On the other hand, depending on where you live, you might see 30 or 40 minutes as better than nothing. In my own case, I have a burn at the bottom of my garden with small brownies, a shoreline less than 10 minutes away and, with a following wind, I could just about walk to a choice of two trout fisheries in 15 minutes and squeeze in half an hour's fluff-chucking.

I did include the information in my first column after the lockdown but didn't make a big deal of it because police contacts were telling me officers had been instructed to stop people fishing. The last thing I wanted was folk getting into bother with the cops because I'd given them the OK.

So, just four days in and already a pattern of mixed messages and lack of clarity was emerging.

APRIL 10. *On his bike.*

NEARLY three weeks into lockdown and a big moment, this time involving an old pal who is a politician, as in a proper, elected parliamentary politician. He was out on his bike for his daily exercise when he stopped to text me in his usual no-frills, no-pleasantries, succinct style.

"Thought fisheries were meant to be closed?"

Attached was a picture he had just taken of a commercial trout water not just open but in full swing, a group of anglers bunched into a corner where they probably thought they wouldn't be spotted from the main road.

I had been under no illusions that there would be individual anglers breaking the rules and carrying on fishing even if, to my knowledge anyway, they hadn't yet got to the stage of blatantly and defiantly posting about it on social media. By this time, I had also heard whispers about a couple of fisheries still operating on the quiet.

But this photo was way beyond rumour. This was hard, unambiguous evidence and it wasn't just a lone, rogue rule breaker. This was an organised, business-as-usual day at a fishery. It felt like a real choker, especially as I had been telling anyone of influence who would listen how responsible the angling community had been since lockdown started.

More than that though, the fact the tip had come from a politician had me already fearing there would be repercussions for our sport down the line.

MAY 1. *Fishery wars.*

SIX weeks in and the simmering tensions between a number of trout fisheries were about to boil over. You could see it coming. The moans, the sniping, the he-said, she-said rows, the whispers about who was operating on the sly. Frustration and resentment, threats and bust-ups…if there had been fly-on-the-wall cameras, the fishery feuds could have replaced the soaps when they ran out of episodes.

Stories circulated about cops chucking anglers off one

223

fishery, another place even holding competitions. Folk were sending me screen grabs of private messages, supposedly from fishery owners, telling regulars to come along discretely for a session, even advising them where to park their cars so they wouldn't be spotted by prying eyes.

I largely ignored it all because when you have worked in newspapers for 40-odd years, your nose can usually tell gossip from fact. I know the difference between the evidence needed to go to print and useless tittle-tattle. I also know how easy it is to fake just about anything in the computer age.

On this issue, I was acutely aware that much of the information, or misinformation, was coming from people with a vested interest and their own agenda.

But the game changed dramatically when one fishery owner put his head above the parapet and announced that he was going to break the lockdown and reopen. In a declaration of defiance, he invited anglers to book slots for day and evening sessions but warned: "I'm positive the police will turn up and we might be asked to leave."

Within a couple of days, he had backtracked, insisting he had only been trying to start a conversation and had suffered the wrath of other fishery owners for his trouble. He claimed he had received death threats and warnings of violence against his family. It was a classic PR recovery trick – when you mess up, turn yourself into the victim.

After his initial announcement, another fishery boss issued a passionate statement, saying that opening during the lockdown would be irresponsible and an insult to virus victims. He warned he would report anyone who did so to the police. Yet another very experienced fishery owner weighed in, using incendiary language like *evil* and *death camp* to describe any venue that started operating before the lockdown was lifted.

Knockabout stuff like this is a gift to journalists but I took no pleasure in it because I knew by then that the main angling organisations were lobbying behind the scenes to try and make sure fishing would be at the head of the queue when restrictions were eased. I had been consulted second-hand myself so I knew how delicate the situation was. This kind of vicious infighting would not help our cause one bit.

On the other hand, I couldn't simply ignore it so I decided I would try to knock heads together in my column that week, laying out all the claims and counter claims. There are two things I need to make clear. First, I was breaking no exclusive secrets when I published that column. Every single, sorry episode I relayed had already been played out in full, gory detail in public – I simply pulled it all together into chronological order. Second, crucially, I used no names, either of fisheries or individuals. I still haven't even now.

My aim was to replace the unseemly feuding with mutual support and solidarity, not to embarrass anyone. I was also wary of playing into the burgeoning vigilante culture – right across society, not just in fishing – that made me every bit as uncomfortable as those breaking the rules.

But one fishery owner then took matters into their own hands by naming the people and places they assumed my column had been about. Then, having outed themselves and named others, the same person accused me of getting them kicked out of angling groups and leaving them open to criticism.

I have been around the block enough times not to let this kind of stuff bother me. I've seen the shoot-the-messenger frenzy a thousand times. As I've told the journalism students I now teach at university, the first requirement for a columnist is to grow several layers of thick skin. Your job is to shine a light on topics and take a view. If you put your name – and your face – on what you write, you can expect folk to take a pop. They've paid for the paper so it is their right. All you can do is stick to your guns and wind yourself up to do it all again next time.

In this case, I like to think that once the dust settled, the whole situation did calm down a little. Most of the warring social media posts, written in frustration or haste or anger or desperation, were quietly removed and replaced by an air of conciliation and preparation for the *new normal,* which became the buzz phrase. For my part, I just kept looking forward to the day when I could get back to writing about actual fishing.

MAY 11. *Too little too late.*

THE tale of the salmon river in North-East Scotland gave me a real jolt because it came so late in the game, seven weeks after the start of lockdown and when the finishing line was already in sight. A local angling association issued an astonishing statement reminding members that when they bought their permits, they were advised that they could fish safely as long as they stuck to social distancing and, I quote, *well up the river away from the general population.*

In other words, stay out of sight, keep your heads down and you'll be fine. Just so there is no confusion, this was an established fishing club giving its members advice on how to break the regulations.

But the situation had changed, the association now explained, after they received complaints from the public. Basically, they had been rumbled. Their statement concluded: "Having considered these requests and the strength of opposition, the proprietors of the river consider the complaints justified. We admit to an error of judgement in this matter and ask all anglers to refrain from fishing until further notice."

Error of judgement? Yeah, sure. Anyone else seriously believe they would have owned up to it if they hadn't been caught?

The story of this angling club, along with the fishery pic texted by my MSP pal, left me disillusioned. The feeling wasn't helped by persistent messages I had been receiving about one particular trout fishery which had continued to open. I have known the owner for a few years so I asked him straight out and he put his hands up, insisting it had been a one-off, though I later heard several reports to the contrary.

My experience of anglers and people in the fishing business is that the overwhelming majority are decent, friendly, helpful, honest and easy to deal with. I still believe that and I have numerous examples of folk looking out for each other during the lockdown. But here was a whole sub-section of anglers sneaking around while everybody else was doing the right thing.

I wasn't naïve. I knew from the start there would be some individuals who would decide the rules didn't apply to them and whose consciences wouldn't be troubled by breaking them. There always are. But now I was seeing evidence of the odd business and club taking the mickey out of the rest of us.

At the same time, those who had flouted the regulations from the off were now growing bolder, rubbing it in everyone else's faces by openly posting reports and pics of their catches.

Towards the end of lockdown, the debate had moved way beyond the rights and wrongs of fishing, almost as if there was an acceptance that people were now doing their own thing and to hell with everyone else. The whole argument shifted 180 degrees into a declaration of war on grassing, as if the real bad guys weren't those going fishing but anyone who dared dob them in.

A growing number of vicious rants appeared against those who were shaming the rule breakers on social media. The attitude of defiance was ramped up by threats against bailiffs who seized fishing gear from offenders, with dire warnings from some, like "they'll get my gutting knife up their hole".

It was a culture that said reporting the crime was much worse than doing the crime.

It deeply saddened me that after years of fighting the corner of all anglers, I ended up feeling a disconnect with a minority who either thought they knew better or were too selfish too care. All around us, real people were dying on the frontline of what we kept hearing was a war. Giving up fishing for a couple of months was hardly the biggest sacrifice anyone had ever been asked to make.

MAY 15. *The pike puzzle.*

THE coronavirus restrictions had been in place for eight weeks when a particularly big Loch Lomond pike was entered into the Prize Catch contest in my Scottish Sun column. Prize Catch, incidentally, is just fish of the week by another name. I called it that to avoid confusion with a rival paper's competition but even after 12 years, everyone calls it *fish of the week* anyway.

My immediate reaction was that this pike looked almost freakishly large which raised the first warning flag. It put me in mind of pics I have seen of muskies, those fearsome pike-cousins that lurk in the giant lakes of Canada and America's northern states. I came to the conclusion that it was either a seriously huge specimen or else it had been photoshopped. What, you don't believe that kind of thing goes on?

I read the guy's email further...reel screaming, 10-minute fight on a kiddie's rod, fish jumping, shock at the size etc etc. Then he mentioned there was a really good video of the catch so I thought, perfect, that will clear it up because if this is genuine, it's definitely going in the paper. The clip was a let-down, ultimately, like a sighting of Nessie or a UFO.

There were tantalising glimpses of the pike as it was being played and yes, it was obviously a good fish but just how good was impossible to tell. There was too much glare, the fish didn't show itself for long enough and, like the end of a telly episode that leaves you hanging, the video stopped just before it was landed. When I asked why, I was told it was because the fish wouldn't fit in the net so two anglers had to lift it and couldn't hold their mobile at the same time.

Hmm, feasible, I supposed, but if I was Sherlock, I'd still

be pacing the room in my deerstalker, puffing furiously on a pipe. There was another question I had asked twice which hadn't been answered so I pressed him again. *When was the fish caught?* Finally, he came back with April 25. *What, during the lockdown?* Yeah, he replied, but didn't elaborate.

At this point, I need to explain that when the lockdown started, I had to quickly figure out if I could maintain a fishing column when there was no actual fishing going on or at least nothing authorised. Now, before you think the obvious, of course I knew there were much more vital issues to worry about in a global pandemic. But actually, recreational activities like fishing and golf – and sport generally – are important during times of crisis. They can act like an oasis of relief amongst all the angst and trauma. They can also serve as beacons of hope, something to look forward to and cling on to during the worst of times.

Filling the main story part of the column was simple. It's something I am trained for. When newspapers have barren spells on the horizon, like the news desert between Christmas and New Year, or the month every two years when Scotland are not at a major football tournament while our neighbours are, the self-starter part of the brain goes into automatic overdrive. You come up with ideas for stories and features to fill the inevitable blanks and, invariably, you end up overcompensating. By close of play on the day when the politicians ordered us to stay indoors – or, to be honest, a few days before because we all saw it coming – I had about 10 weeks' worth of columns mapped out.

But there was still the Prize Catch competition to sort out

because that is the column's shop window, the movie trailer, the concert poster. However much my ego would like to think that it's my carefully crafted words that count, I'm realistic enough to accept it's the weekly winning fish that pulls in the punters. Then, with a bit of luck, they hang around long enough to read at least the first few sentences of my main article.

Prize Catch is sponsored by Scottish-based tackle giants Daiwa, with whom I have had an excellent relationship dating back a dozen years. They laid on a big-money giveaway for my opening column in March 2008, didn't hesitate when I gave them first refusal on Prize Catch and we backed the Carron Valley Masters together for a number of years. They were of the same mind as me about lockdown – that we should keep the competition going as a morale booster for anglers.

I already had a decent backlog of entries and supplemented that by inviting readers to send in fish they had caught before the lockdown and to resubmit ones from the previous year that might have fallen through the net, pardon the pun. But I made it clear in my column every Friday as long as restrictions lasted – any fish entered had to be caught BEFORE the lockdown which ruled out the Loch Lomond pike, no matter how impressive.

When I told the guy that I couldn't use it in the paper, his response was what became a common theme in debates on the rights and wrongs of going fishing while restrictions were in force.

"We're not the only ones though. Check the River Kelvin out – you'll see loads of people fishing and the police don't even stop them or crack a light."

It's the old two-wrongs-make-a-right justification, akin to seeing other folk driving at 100mph on a motorway so that makes it OK for you to do the same thing. Not a defence I would recommend using in a court of law.

In the end, Loch Lomond man acknowledged he shouldn't have been out fishing and graciously stepped back with a "doesny matter" parting shot.

But wait, I've kept the worst bit till last, the bit that really depressed me. What I haven't told you is that in his original email, the guy told me the huge pike had been one of 18 landed that day, then added: "We caught 53 pike in three weeks up there – the fishing has been unreal, no joke, even on Flying Cs."

I think that might have been my lowest fishing point of the lockdown, like someone giving the rest of us the fingers, ripping it right out of us. Having the time of their lives, filling their boots, being smarter than us saps doing the right thing and watching Tiger King for the third time while they're having a pike fest to themselves.

Another thing, I also didn't like how it made me feel – the resentment that festered deep down inside because there will almost certainly be no consequences for these guys. Thinking like that is not who I am and I resent them doubly for turning me into someone who would relish raw revenge.

MAY 22. *Morning person.*

WELCOME to Day 60 of the lockdown but it could just as easily be Day 7 or Day 23 or Day 49 because the nice lady from the fishery at the top of the hill does exactly what she has been doing every morning since we were all told to stay at home for our own safety. She posts pictures on

Facebook, often of rising fish, sometimes scenic views from her lofty vantage point, occasionally one of her breakfast. She adds some good tunes as a backing track, then says *Good Morning* to a growing band of people – anglers, family and other friends.

I'm not sure if the nice lady herself was fully aware of the power and the value of the Senga Murray Good Morning Club.

No question there was a stack of negatives about the lockdown, fishing ones included, but we must not forget the many good people who did good things. For starters, there were those who run our fishing organisations – often maligned – quietly lobbying the Government on our behalf.

On a more down to earth level, you had folk discretely keeping an eye on others who weren't coping so well with isolation. Giving them a call every now and then, sending them the odd text, sharing daft clips of piano-playing geese. There were amateur fly tiers finding the confidence to put pics and clips of their creations online for the first time, others posting snaps from old fishing adventures, a few making up quizzes.

OK, we all eventually got fed up being asked for 10 album covers and how many rabbits were carrying carrots across the river but at least they were a diversion. They took our tormented minds away from the crisis and the loneliness for a little while at least.

That is what was so important and so genius about Senga's bright and breezy start to each day. From the banks of New Haylie fishery, she single-handedly built a sense of community, gave folk a lift just when the thought of getting out of bed and facing another long, shapeless day was dragging them down. She was reminding people that they weren't going through this alone and, vitally, offering a glimpse of what was waiting when we came out the other side.

I have been a tabloid journalist for most of my career and I know that what sells papers – or nowadays gets clicks – is a diet of scandal, sex, outrage, tragedy, hostility and horror. But I have never forgotten that you have to sprinkle fun, quirkiness, glamour, sport and showbiz into the mix. In newspapers we called it light and shade.

There has been and continues to be more than enough shade to endure throughout the coronavirus nightmare but the light has come from Senga and all the other unsung fishing heroes.

JUNE 2. *Back in action.*
THIS week I have been out fishing. How often do you get to write that in a fishing column and it actually means something? Yes, it was the great escape to the banks, shores and boats with catch returns and rod averages through the roof. When I saw some of the numbers – 75 in a day for one fly angler – I felt sorry for all those fish that had been lulled into a false sense of security. Fish that must have thought they had been transported to a watery rest home to live out their lives in peace, with no one to disturb them.

But apart from a condensed version of what it must feel like to be set free after being banged up for a crime you didn't commit, what did we learn from the end of lockdown? Well, nothing we didn't already know, as it turns out. Was anyone really surprised to learn that the vast majority of anglers are good, sensible folk who instinctively do the right thing and stick to the rules?

When we got the green light to go back out fishing, I didn't hear of one bit of bother at commercial venues, or at canals or harbours or salmon beats. We were grateful to get our fishing back and valued it too much to risk having it taken away again.

So impeccable was the conduct that most fishery bosses very quickly confirmed social distancing was second nature in our sport and that they didn't need to be too strict about making folk book in advance. Anglers also showed they were smart enough to know that if they turned up at a place and found it crowded, there were plenty of other spots to choose from.

Like so many other people, health issues meant I had to be cautious so I waited a few extra days to avoid both the first-day stampede and the weekend rush. Luckily for me, I'm spoiled for choice with so many excellent trout waters all genuinely local, not to mention miles of seashore within walking distance.

When I did venture out with fly rod, the virus wasn't an issue, aside from reaching into my pocket for Gink and pulling out hand-sanitiser. I chose a place I knew would be relatively quiet and was still able to chat to other anglers without having to see the whites of their eyes.

As for the fishing itself, you know how folk sometimes say they're happy to just be out and don't care if they catch? Usually no one believes them but that is honestly how I felt because it was all about the freedom to wander and enjoy open spaces.

On a day of muggy, sapping heat, the trout were down deep and lethargic. I figured it would be like when a football team play tough opposition and know they'll only get a couple of chances so they need to take them. That was pretty much how it worked out. Three hours, six offers, four hooked, three in the net.

I went home pretty damn delighted just to be back out there. Getting to feel a tug on my line was a bonus. At the end of the day, as long as you can get out fishing and yes, maybe catch the odd one, nothing much else really matters.

Same as it always was. Same as it always will be.

Chapter 18

Don't look now

AS a reward for sticking with the book all the way to the final chapter, I've kept the best till last. Get ready because this is a biggie.

I am now going to reveal to you an iron-cast, one thousand per cent certain way to catch more fish. Before I do though, there is a snag. In order to let you into the secret that will transform your fishing and change your life forever, I need to break a promise. At the very beginning, right there in the introduction, I declared that this was not a How-To book. Remember?

My thinking was simple. Aspiring writers will always get the same advice – stick to what you know, play to your strengths. So, I set out to do what I've been doing in newspapers for more than 40 years – tell stories in a clear, interesting and, hopefully, entertaining way. That was the plan and it was going OK, I think.

But since starting to write this book, I have stumbled upon a revolutionary, foolproof new method of fishing. So confident am I that this method cannot fail, that if it was in my power (which it isn't) I would offer you a money-back guarantee. And yes, I suppose you could fairly argue that you have heard the same kind of boasts from door-to-door double glazing salesmen and backstreet car dealers, not to mention those nice folk who take the time and trouble to write to you from Spain, or sometimes Nigeria, asking if you would mind them parking their £48million fortune in your bank and promising to give you half of it for your trouble. Oh, and all you have to do is give them your bank account details. What could possibly go wrong?

But this is different. Come on, you know me. You see my column in the paper every Friday so you know I've got an honest face. I've shared a boat and traded flies with some of you, met loads more of you at fisheries and on rivers, lochs and shores. You know I wouldn't lie to you. OK, OK, turns out I did tell you a tiny porky about this not being a fishing instruction book. But once I unveil this stunning key to certain fishing success, you will not just forgive me but probably name your next-born child or even new dog after me.

First though, this insistence on not writing a How-To book has been bothering me. So let me deal with that before I get on to the good stuff. Even if I did have the necessary expertise – which I don't – I would hesitate to have a go at any kind of fishing manual.

For starters, there are more than enough of them out there already.

Go to the outdoor pursuits or sports section on Amazon or any book store and you will see a whole range of titles offering expert advice on everything from tying shiny flies to catching monster carp to breeding maggots in a box in your wife's shoe cupboard. The last thing you need is another one.

More to the point, there are stacks of anglers and writers who are much better qualified than me to give you advice, whether on the banks or on the shelves. If you are looking for books that will turn you into a better, more informed angler and fly fishing is your game, then let me recommend a couple.

It is hard to believe that it is more than 40 years since Brian Clarke's The Pursuit of Stillwater Trout was first published. The ideas it contains still feel fresh and breakthrough. It was all based on such a simple concept too – the notion that the more you understand about the behaviour of fish and the creatures that form their diet, the better equipped you are to catch them.

There are more light-bulb moments per square inch than you will find in a whole anthology of fishing books. It is also one of the most accessible angling tomes you will come across because it is clear that Clarke was kind of making it up as he went along. He was sharing his own discoveries with the wonder of a child and without resorting to jargon because it felt like he hadn't learned – or maybe invented – the jargon himself yet.

Just as enlightening and perhaps even more relevant if you do the bulk of your trout chasing north of the border, is

The Loch Fisher's Bible, by Stan Headley.

It takes a heap of confidence to call a book the bible of anything but Stan backs it up with profound knowledge and forensic methodology. He even pulls off the neat trick of encapsulating pretty much all you need to know about fly fishing in Scotland in a single page. (Page 169 if you're in a rush.)

I was a few years into my second incarnation as a fly angler when this came out in 2005 and reading it made me mentally clear the decks and reshape my whole thinking about catching trout.

If you prefer to do your learning by watching, hunt down some of Paul Young's old Hooked on Scotland and Hooked on Fishing shows – there are plenty of them kicking around the interweb. OK, entertainment value had to be a priority but you don't maintain such a big reputation 20 years after the event without knowing your stuff.

He also happens to be a very nice guy – a genuine what you see is what you get character, helpful and gracious whenever our paths have crossed.

But enough of this plugging other anglers, let's get back to the revolutionary new method of mine that is going to transform your fishing forever.

Actually, let's not go there quite yet because at this point I am duty bound to admit that this is not the first time I have discovered what I was convinced was going to be the method that changed the face of fishing, became my legacy and ensured my angling immortality.

I had even started dreaming that long after I had gone to that trout-filled loch in the sky, anglers would be whispering my name in hushed, reverent tones as they yet again turned to the Kernan Katch trick and gave a little smile. (Now that I think about it, the name probably needed a little work.) That first idea turned into a false start, admittedly, but when I explain it you will understand why I was so convinced I was on to something.

This was around the time when I had been giving an awful lot of thought to how to select the right fly when trout are on the rise. I had reached the stage where I had become fed up envying all those anglers who seemed to know intuitively what fly to tie on when they arrived at the loch or the river so I spent a lot of time studying and even did a bit of homework. I know now that it's stating the obvious in a Homer Simpson *D'oh!* kind of way but after a little while the penny dropped that my eyes were the best starting point.

To be honest, I have never got round to making a close study of creepy-crawlies and I have long forgotten most of the Latin I learned at secondary school. That means I am not clued up on the big words for tiny insects. But a little bit of casual study should give you an inkling as to what bugs are in the water and in the air. You don't need to be an entomological expert to come to the conclusion that if the fish are taking wee black stuff, you should probably go find something in your fly box that resembles wee black stuff.

(Or, sometimes, the exact opposite because trout can be contrary creatures. I once nearly drove myself mad trying to match the minute bugs the fish were gorging on a loch in Galloway till a local turned up, took a quick look, chucked out a big Daddy and caught two in five minutes.)

Once you've done your best to replicate the natural menu, you can venture down the more technical route of

241

checking the rise forms for clues about what stage the hatch is at. Like if the fish are just breaking the surface with their backs and tails, you can guess they're probably on emergers, i.e., beasties that haven't quite made it to the top. Then there's the dimpling, spreading circles which indicate trout are feeding on the surface or maybe a fraction below it, not forgetting the more violent, slashing explosions that suggest there are bigger bugs around which are making the fish aggressive and reckless. That's when I'd be reaching for the Daddies and Sedgehogs.

So yes, you can consider all that scientific stuff to guide your fly selection. Or, and this is where I thought I had cracked fishing's Da Vinci Code first time round, you can take your cue from a bit of ordinary, supermarket kitchen roll.

Let me explain. I was enjoying a very fruitful afternoon at one of my favourite small stillwaters. I had been there for maybe three hours and I'd caught a dozen or so of the top-grade trout that are stocked regularly. My fishing diary reminds me that my catch was split pretty much 50-50 between a Black Shuttlecock on the tail and a Spider on the dropper. Top sport and great fun. As a way of passing an afternoon, you couldn't ask for much more.

There had been a bit of a lull in the action for half an hour or so and the Shuttlecock had become sodden and bedraggled so I squeezed it dry with a piece of kitchen roll that I always keep in my pocket for just that purpose. A tiny corner of the white material broke off, blew on to the water and, well, there are no prizes for guessing what happened next.

It was engulfed with such speed and ferocity that I tore

off another scrap and let it blow out of my fingers just in case I'd come across a crazed but one-off cannibal trout with a penchant for cleaning materials. But no, the same thing happened again. (Sorry for polluting your water.)

I might be slow on the uptake but even I can take a hint now and again. On went a Size 14 bushy white version of the Yellow Owl that I told you about in an earlier chapter, the fly I get a regular supply of from Iona Allan – aka The Fly Lady – over at Allandale Tarn in West Lothian.

What followed was the most frantic spell of surface action I have ever encountered in all my years of fishing. For the next hour and a half, the trout took a mad turn, shoving each other aside to get their jaws around the fly. Every single cast, without exception, produced a fish or at least a vicious slash at the Owl within seconds of it hitting the water. I had to change the fly twice to replace the battered and tattered old ones.

In that incredible 90-minute spell, I caught 25 trout and know that I missed or dropped at least the same again. I also got seriously filthy looks from the bloke on the far bank even though I'd shouted over what I was catching on at an early stage in the feeding frenzy.

I can be exact about the timescale because I was fishing to a deadline that day. On principle, this is something that all leisure fishers should avoid. Competition anglers, fair enough, because matches need to have a start time and a finish time. But if you are fishing to relax, ideally you should leave your watch at home or at least in the car and pack up when you feel like it. That said, if it comes down to fishing on the clock or not at all, I'll take it.

On that particular day, I had arranged to fish till 7pm, be

home for half past and ready to set out by eight for the drive north to visit our oldest daughter. Despite my best efforts to slow down time, it got to five past seven – we can always explain away five minutes – and I found myself calling my wife, begging to be allowed to stay out playing for an extra quarter of an hour like a little kid.

Yes, I thought, I've cracked it. An honest to goodness eureka moment. An actual original discovery. I could become known as the guy who invented a completely new technique. I started to wonder if I could get a kitchen roll manufacturer to sponsor my fishing column until I realised I didn't know the names of any. My wife was right – again. I do walk around the supermarket with my eyes glued to my phone.

Of course, you have already guessed that there isn't going to be a happy ending here. It never worked again. I don't mean the fly – Iona's Yellow Owl variant has been a successful staple of mine for years, to the extent that I once bought what must have been almost her entire stock of them.

But the kitchen roll as match-the-hatch sampler? Nah, turned out to be a one-time only deal. Imagine that Stone Age bloke trying to show his mates the wheel and finding he couldn't get it to work properly a second time. *Come back guys, it definitely rolled yesterday, honest.* That's how I felt.

I tried and tried. In the end I had to give up before fisheries banned me for being the weird guy who tried to cover their water in fake snow. I'd like to say that I went through dozens of rolls and different brands but it would only be for dramatic effect.

That is all in the past, though. This new method I have invented is the real deal. It simply cannot fail. Follow it and your catches will increase. I am confident enough not to add any little caveats. Not *should* increase or *might* increase. You *will* catch more fish. No question.

Mind you, think carefully before you go any further. Do you really want to catch more fish? I mean, *really really* want to? That isn't as dumb a question as you think. What if you catch so many that fishing becomes boring? What if there is no challenge any longer?

Picture the scene. You try really hard to use conventional techniques. You try to fish the way you always have in the past where there is a more than decent chance of a reverse Flower of Scotland outcome – you know, the fish come out on top and send you homewards to think again.

But it's always there, the knowledge tucked away in your head that the moment it gets difficult and a dreaded blank starts to loom on the horizon, you can always fall back on Mike's magic method and immediately start catching. Will fishing still be as much fun when failure isn't an option?

If you can honestly answer Yes to that question, then it is probably safe to read on. If you aren't sure, then ask yourself if you possess the self-discipline to use my method only as an occasional treat or when nothing else is working. If you are still saying Yes, then you too can keep reading. If you are the type of angler who has too many days when you don't catch at all, then you most definitely want to read on because in just a few moments, you will possess the knowledge that will confine soul-destroying fishless sessions to a thing of the past.

This technique is so deadly that it would be a crime not to share it with you. It is also so simple and obvious that once you read about it, you will be amazed that no one has ever thought of it before, or if they have, taken it seriously.

Now, I like all kinds of fishing. I find it difficult to pass any body of water, be it fresh or salty, without stopping for a look and weighing up its angling potential. I would fish in a puddle with a stick and a pin.

But I make no secret of the fact that fly fishing is what floats my boat more than any other branch off the sport. I am explaining this because it was for fly fishing – and dry flies in particular – that this method was developed and honed.

That said, I am supremely confident it will work in just about every kind of fishing. For match and predator anglers, it will most definitely work when you are using floats. Likewise, any kind of sea angling that requires concentration and fast, firm reaction. The method will also easily adapt to spinning.

I've not really settled on a name for this fantastic new technique. Obviously, I'm far too modest to do it myself but if anglers who adopt it decide to call it the Marvellous Mike Kernan Method, then I'd be proud to be recognised and, ultimately, remembered in that way.

OK, here goes, and you might want to take notes. It is no exaggeration to say that this will be the most important piece of fishing advice you will ever receive.

Just stop for a moment and think of all the times when you look away while you are supposed to be concentrating on your fly – or float, or line, or spinner. It could be as simple as another angler walking past and asking if you are catching much. You would have to take rudeness to new levels not to turn and exchange a few words. So yes, the distraction caused by human contact could be key to this revolutionary technique.

What else? Well, a major part of fishing is about being in the big outdoors immersed in all that nature so what takes your attention away from the business at hand momentarily could be a deer racing down the hill to your left, or a bird of prey hovering overhead as it prepares to swoop on its hapless prey, or an industrious rabbit mooching about in the gorse bushes on your right before returning to its burrow for some good loving.

It could be something much more mundane, like reaching to get a Mars Bar out of your pocket, checking your watch, reacting to the beep or vibration of a text or football scores alert.

Of course, it could be a distraction more directly connected to the fishing itself. Who, for example, can possibly resist reacting and turning their head to the splash or disturbance of a rising or leaping fish? (I hate to make wild accusations but I have started to suspect that certain fishery owners train some of their trout to act as decoys, especially when I'm around. You know who you are.)

The point is, and be prepared because I am getting to the big reveal any second, we all know that these are the exact moments when fish will decide to take our fly or bait.

You see? Is there a single angler out there who has not just seen the light and is even now bathed in a shaft of dazzling recognition?

Think of all those times you curse when you turn away for a split second and out of the corner of your eye you see that telltale flurry around your fly, or the float vanish momentarily, or the boat rod take a sudden wrench.

And even in that instant when you see or feel it happen, you already knew it is too late and the fish has been and gone. It has spat out your March Brown, your maggot, your mackerel strip or whatever. Already it is laughing at you, using its fins to high-five the mate who performed the dummy rise and telling the rest of the shoal what a sucker you are.

So rather than cursing these moments and dismissing them as angling's version of sods law, it dawned on me that we should create them on purpose and harness them. Pretend to look away but sneakily keep one eye squinting at your fly or float. If that doesn't work, look away for no more than two or three seconds then jerk your head back round swiftly to spot the take and react to it. I'm even thinking of refining it, taking it a step further and getting little mirrors fitted to my fishing bunnet.

So, there it is. Couldn't be simpler. The Look Away Method. Your fishing future is now assured. When you are the envy of the fishery or the boat, remember where you heard it first.

Printed in Great Britain
by Amazon